SPAIN
Practical Commercial Law

SPAIN
Practical Commercial Law

SUSANA MIRANDA
Spanish Lawyer, LLM

GENERAL EDITOR
ALEXIS MAITLAND HUDSON
Avocat à la cour
Solicitor

© Longman Group Ltd 1993

Published by
Longman Law, Tax and Finance
Longman Group UK Ltd
21–27 Lamb's Conduit Street
London WC1N 3NJ

Associated offices
Australia, Hong Kong, Malaysia, Singapore, USA

ISBN 085121 7753

Typeset by Servis Filmsetting Ltd, Manchester
Printed and bound in Great Britain by
Biddles Ltd, Guildford and King's Lynn

CONTENTS

INTRODUCTION

The Spanish experience of adopting a democratic system, achieving a balance between central government and regions and introducing substantial changes in the economy has certainly attracted investors. Furthermore, Spain's entry into the EC has emphasised the process of modernisation. This modernisation has certainly reached the legal structure, especially in company/commercial areas. The tools provided by the legal system may be of great assistance to those intending to set up a business in Spain or simply carry out certain activities such as buying or selling property. For those advising their clients in respect of their business decisions an understanding of the legal framework is indispensable.

SOURCES OF LAW

The sources of law of the Spanish system are indicated in art 1 of the Civil Code as legislation, customs and general principles of law. Within the term *legislation*, is included a variety of laws with different status, the most important being the Spanish Constitution of 1978. The Constitution is followed by other laws called organic laws (*leyes organicas*) which deal with fundamental civil rights and liberties and other matters as stated in the Spanish Constitution (art 81). These laws are followed in order by the ordinary laws (*leyes ordinarias*) and various types of decree (*decretos*). Article 82 of the Constitution provides that the Parliament 'may delegate to the government the power to issue rules with the force of law on specific matters'. In addition, in accordance with art 86, the government may pass temporary legislative provisions in cases of extraordinary and urgent need. These provisions take the form of decree-laws and are subject to several restrictions: for example, they may not affect the rights, duties and liberties contained in Title I of the Constitution

('Concerning Fundamental Rights and Duties'). These decree-laws must be submitted forthwith to the Congress of Deputies, which must approve them or reject them within 30 days of promulgation. This principle of the hierarchy of laws is stated in art 1–2 of the Civil Code, which provides that those laws which conflict with the provisions of other laws higher in the hierarchy will be void.

The Civil Code also gives the general rules as to custom, which is applied only if no applicable law exists and provided that it does not offend morality or is not contrary to public order. In the event that there is no applicable law or custom, the general principles of law may be taken into account. This is without prejudice to the fact that general principles of law are considered as forming part of the whole of the legal system. For example, this is the case with the principle of freedom to contract, which is restricted only by law, morality and public order.

The Spanish Constitution provides the basis of the Spanish political system and provides the fundamental principles for the government, the Congress of Deputies and the Senate which forms the Parliament (*Cortes Generales*), and the judiciary. The government is responsible for the political direction of the state. The Parliament is entrusted with the legislative power of the state including the approval of the budget, and also control of the actions of the executive. The judiciary are entrusted with the application of the law in all proceedings in accordance with the rules of jurisdiction and judicial proceedings.

The Constitution provides the basis of a political balance between being a unified state and also a country divided into 17 autonomous regions. The regions are given certain powers to legislate, to have their own government, their own courts and also their own local authorities. These powers are dealt with by the Constitution in Chapter 3 and also in various other provisions of the Constitution such as, for example, art 2 in which is stated:

'The Constitution is based on the indissoluble unity of the Spanish nation, the common and indivisible country of all Spaniards; it recognises and guarantees the right of autonomy of the nationalities and regions of which it is composed, and solidarity amongst them all'; and in art 3.2, 'the other Spanish languages shall also be official for the autonomous communities in accordance with the statutes'.

As to the legal system in general, it is a civil law system, so that legislation and customs are applied by the courts but court decisions are not considered as sources of law, although it is generally accepted that they provide guidelines in respect of the application and interpretation of the law.

COURTS AND PROCEEDINGS

The Spanish Constitution deals with the judiciary in Title VI (arts 117 to 127). Jurisdiction of the courts is subdivided into four groups: civil, criminal, administrative and labour. There is a hierarchy of courts, with the bottom tier being the justice of the peace courts (*Juzgados de Paz*) which have jurisdiction in respect of minor criminal and civil matters, and the top tier, the Supreme Court (*Tribunal Supremo*), which is the highest court in respect of all matters apart from those cases which are dealt with specifically by the Constitutional Court. The Supreme Court has, therefore, jurisdiction to deal with civil, criminal, administrative, labour and military matters. Jurisdiction of the courts is defined by the Judiciary Law of 1985 (*Ley Organica del Poder Judicial*) which specifies the matters over which Spanish courts have jurisdiction (art 22). In addition, arts 8 to 12 of the Civil Code provide the general rules as to private international law. The Judiciary Law also governs the organisation and administration of the courts.

As to the types of proceedings, it should be stated that under Spanish law there is a variety of proceedings available depending on the type of claim submitted, so that there are for example, civil and commercial proceedings, criminal proceedings, administrative proceedings, and labour proceedings.

Foreign judgments may be enforced in Spain. Articles 951 *et seq* of the Civil Procedure Law establish that foreign judgments will be enforced in Spain in accordance with the international treaties entered into by Spain. If there is no applicable treaty, recognition may be obtained by means of a special procedure through the Supreme Court (*exequatur*). In connection with multilateral treaties, Spain has ratified the Brussels Convention on Jurisdiction and the Enforcement of Judgments in Civil and Commercial Matters. In addition, Spain is also a party to other Conventions such as for example, the Convention on the service abroad of judicial and extra-judicial documents in civil or commercial matters (the 'Hague Convention').

THE LEGAL PROFESSION

Lawyers (*Abogados*)

These undertake to defend the interest of their clients in accordance with codes of ethics. The Spanish General Council for the Legal Profession has adopted the code of ethics for European Community Lawyers. Those who wish to practice the legal profession must be law graduates and must join a bar association as a practising member. In addition to providing their clients with legal advice, lawyers are also able to appear before courts on behalf of their clients, whether they are plaintiffs or defendants.

Court Representatives (*Procuradores*)

These are responsible for representing clients before the courts. They act by means of a power of attorney which must be granted specifically for these purposes. They liaise between the courts and the lawyers. They are also organised through associations and as in the case of lawyers, owe a duty of confidentiality to their clients.

Notaries (*Notarios Publicos*)

These professionals are entrusted with the drafting of documents. They keep the original copies of such documents and issue copies attesting to their content and to the authenticity of the facts stated in them. All documents issued by the notaries must be signed by them and also have their seal affixed. Notaries' licences are issued by the Ministry of Justice after they have passed a very competitive examination as the places are limited and they are appointed in respect of some specific area. There are many legal transactions in Spain which require a deed to be authenticated before a public notary, such as, those to be submitted to some official registries. There are three public registries in Spain, these being the Land Registry, the Commercial Registry and the Civil Registry. In addition, there are several administrative registries such as the Industrial Properties Registry and the Intellectual Properties Registry.

1
INDUSTRIAL AND INTELLECTUAL PROPERTY

1.1 PATENTS

1.1.1 FILING PROCEDURE

The most important rules dealing with patents in Spain are the Spanish Patent Law of 20 March 1986 (11/86) which has been in force since 25 June 1986 and the Royal Decree 2245/1986 implementing it. Title II of the Patent Law contains provisions stating the requirements for patenting an invention. Articles 4 and 5 are particularly important in that Article 4 indicates, in general terms, new inventions which are innovative and of significant industrial application which can be patented while art 5 excludes some specific categories from being patented. Article 5, for example, excludes:

(a) animals;
(b) plants which are protected by the law dated 12 March 1975; and
(c) inventions whose publication or exploitation are contrary to the public order or morality.

Article 4 also excludes certain categories which cannot be properly considered as inventions. These include:

(a) discoveries, scientific theories and mathematical methods;
(b) literary, artistic, scientific and other intellectual works; and
(c) a method or manner for presenting information.

Patents may be registered in Spain without many difficulties. Title V of the Law deals with the application and procedure.

The application for registration, on the official application form, is submitted to the Director of the Registry of Industrial Property (*Registro de la Propiedad Industrial*). It must comply with the requirements of the Patent Law, which, specifies the documents to be attached. These include:

(a)   a description of the invention;

(b)   drawings relating to the description or to the claims made;

(c)   a summary of the invention;

(d)   payment of the application fee; and

(e)   other relevant documents of the particular application such as authorisation granted in favour of a patent agent.

The most important documents forming part of the application are the description of the invention and the claims made. Article 25 of the Patent Law requires that the description should be sufficiently clear and complete for an expert to be able to put it into practice. As to the claims, these will provide the basis of the rights eventually granted by registration of the patent. The application must be in a Spanish language. However, an application from a Spanish region may be in the official language of the region, accompanied by a translation into Spanish.

The Registry of Industrial Property will examine the application and may require amendments, which have to be dealt with within a period of two months.

If the application is successful, the grant of the patent must be published in the official Industrial Properties Gazette, with details of the patent including description and drawings. In practice, the party interested in proceeding with a registration will appoint an agent, by means of a power of attorney. This power of attorney will contain the details of the grantor, the agent and the description of the patent (or utility model). A power of attorney should be widely drawn so that the agent will be able to deal with any opposition which may be filed against the application. Normally this power of attorney does not need to be legally authenticated.

The validity of a patent, once granted, may be challenged in the ordinary courts.

1.1.2   PROTECTION AND REVOCATION

Protection

Patents are valid for 20 years non-renewable from the date of submission of the application. Patent holders are required to pay annual fees to the Registry of Industrial Property and to exploit the invention, either themselves or through an authorised person.

Article 50 of the Law outlines the general rights of the holder of a patent, which, broadly, are to prevent a third party from doing any specified acts without consent. The prohibited activities are as follows:

(a) the manufacture, sale, use or possession of the patented product; or

(b) using or marketing the patented procedure provided that the third party is aware of the patent or of using a product obtained through the patented procedure.

Article 51 also gives rights to prevent a third party from providing unauthorised parties with the means of producing the invention.

The following remedies are available to patent holders under Article 62 of the Patent Law to protect their rights:

(a) an injunction to restrain further violation of the rights;

(b) compensation for damage resulting from infringements;

(c) the seizure of goods produced or transmitted in violation of the rights;

(d) further measures to prevent future infringements, including destruction of the seized goods.

Legal proceedings may be initiated by the holder of a patent and also by anyone to whom the patent holder has granted an exclusive licence.

Action must be brought in the ordinary courts within a period of five years, a period which normally runs from the time when the patent holder or his licensee knew of the infringement. Jurisdiction of the court is determined by the defendant's residence. Apart from the general rules of civil procedure the Patent Law includes specific rules as to evidence and interim remedies. The latter may be applied for in order to ensure that the judgment may effectively be enforced (art 133 of the Patent Law).

Revocation

A patent may be revoked on several grounds, for example as the result of a court order. Other grounds are provided in art 116 of the Law, for example, non-payment of the annual fees or non-user of the invention within two years following the grant of the licence. In the event of non-payment, the holder can appeal on the grounds of *force majeure*.

Revocation takes effect when declared by the Registry and published in the Official Gazette (*Boletin Oficial de la Propiedad Industrial*).

1.1.3 UTILITY MODELS

Law 11/86 also contains specific rules applicable to utility models. Under art 143, the concept of utility models includes those new inventions by which an object is given special shape or structure resulting in some important advantage for its use or manufacture. In this category are included instruments, tools and their parts, etc.

Application must be made to the Director of the Registry of Industrial Property. This is done by means of an official form and generally the application procedure is the same as for patents. However, in the case of utility models there is no need to attach a summary of the invention. If the application is successful, it will be published in the Official Gazette. The details of the claims and drawings will also be published. There is a period of two months for third parties to oppose. In the absence of objections, or if these are not upheld, the registration is granted. If objections are lodged, the applicant has one month to amend his application or reply to the objections. After this period the registry will either grant or reject the application, and the decision is duly published in the Official Gazette (*Boletin Oficial de la Propiedad Industrial*). Registrations are valid for a period of ten years and require payment of annual fees.

Article 152 of the Law states that the holders of the registration have the same protection as the holders of registered patents.

1.1.4 EUROPEAN PATENTS

Patent rights may also be obtained through a European application under the European Patent Convention. In order to obtain a patent through this procedure, application in Spanish must be made to the Registry of Industrial Property (*Registro de la Propiedad Industrial*). Applications under the European Patent Convention would normally be submitted by those who intend to exploit a patent in different countries, among them Spain. It is advisable to check the costs in advance, as these may in the end be considerable not only in respect of the registrations but also because of payments of fees for patent renewals.

1.2 TRADE MARKS

1.2.1 APPLICATION AND REGISTRATION

Applicable legislation

Trade marks are generally regulated by Law 32/1988 on Trade Marks, and Royal Decree 645/1990 implementing this law.

Rights in trade marks are given on the basis of registration. However, the owner of a sign clearly known in Spain has the power to challenge a registration within a period of five years of the registration of a mark, on the grounds that it may create confusion in respect of a trade mark previously used.

Article 1 defines a trade mark as a sign or means which distinguishes or is used to distinguish a product or a service, for example (art 2):

(a)   words or a combination of words;
(b)   an image, figures, symbols and graphics;
(c)   letters, numbers and their combinations;
(d)   packaging containers, the shape of a product or its presentation;
(e)   any combination of the above.

Applications must be filed at the Industrial Property Registry (*Registro de la Propiedad Industrial*). Title III of the Law deals with the application procedure, and in particular, art 16 requires the application to include a description (in duplicate) of the trade mark together with a receipt of payment of the relevant fees. As in the case of the patents, all applications should be in Spanish.

There are some specific prohibitions in connection with the registration of trade marks, which may prevent certain trade marks from registration, as for example those which offend against the law, public order or morality, and those which reproduce or imitate flags and other national emblems.

There are also some other relative prohibitions, such as for example:

(a)   marks phonetically or graphically similar to a trade mark previously applied for or registered and relating

to similar or identical products or services and which
might cause a confusion in the market;

(b)   marks that are identical to the name of an establishment which previously applied for or registered a mark
relating to the same activities as those intended for the
trade mark.

Procedure

In practice, before proceeding to apply for a trade mark for
registration, a search is carried out including at least one class of
goods or services. This search is followed by the application
which should include all the classes as appropriate in order to
obtain protection of rights, as discussed below (see 1.2.2).

An applicant is granted preferential rights from the date of
the application which therefore gives protection against third
parties from that date. After the application has been filed, it must
be published in the Official Gazette (*Boletin Oficial de la
Propriedad Industrial*) so that those who consider that their rights
are infringed may oppose the registration within a period of two
months. After this period, the mark is considered for registration
in an Official Examination by the Registrar, who will either
approve the registration, indicate that the application needs to be
amended or reject the application. In the latter case, it is possible
to appeal to the Registrar within one month of the publication of
the refusal of the application in the Official Gazette. All other
appeals and claims are adjudicated by the courts, for example in
the case of an appeal against the final decision of the Registrar.

1.2.2   PROTECTION AND REVOCATION

Protection

The grant of a trade mark is published in the Official Gazette
(*Boletin Oficial de la Propriedad Industrial*). Trade marks are valid
for ten years from the date of the submission of the application,
and are renewable. For purposes of renewal of a mark its use must
be duly declared in a notarial deed.

A trade mark registration gives the holder exclusive rights to
its use. The registration offers protection only in respect of the
class of services or goods indicated in the application, with the
result that a third party may register a similar mark in respect of
different goods or services. In addition, the holder has the right to

claim protection against those violating his rights. Legal action may be taken both in criminal and civil law, to prevent the unauthorised marketing of products identified by a particular trade mark. Interim remedies are available, to obtain the immediate cessation of trade mark infringements. Compensation may be obtained through civil proceedings. The limitation period for civil actions is five years, from the time the injured party could have exercised his rights.

Revocation

Law 32/88 on Trade Marks introduced the requirement that a trade mark must be used, and therefore a trade mark can be revoked if not used for a period of five years, Revocation may be obtained through legal proceedings initiated for these purposes. A trade mark can also be revoked as the result of a judgment declaring that a trade mark is void as being against the provisions of this law, or on other grounds such as, for example, non-payment of the fees which are due every five years.

1.2.3 TRADING AND COMMERCIAL NAMES (*NOMBRES COMERCIALES Y ROTULOS DE ESTABLECIMIENTOS*)

Trading names include those symbols or names which are used to identify a company or a person for purposes of business and which distinguish their activities from that of others which may be similar or identical. Article 76 of Law 32/88 on Trade Marks lists by way of example:

(a) a family name, firm name or company name;
(b) an anagram;
(c) a name relating to the object of the business etc.

Commercial names may also be registered and the same name can be used for chain stores in one or more municipal districts. If a commercial name is to be used as a trade mark the name and the trade mark must be registered separately and simultaneously. The name in the case of trading names may also be:

(a) a family name;
(b) a firm name or a company name;
(c) an anagram and other combinations as stated in Article 82.

In general terms it can be stated that there is no special requirements and that any symbol which is useful to identify a physical or corporate person in a business may be used.

The rules relating to the application and registration procedure of trade marks (see 1.2.1 above) also apply to trading and commercial names.

1.2.4 UNFAIR COMPETITION

The Law on Trade Marks gives a general definition of unfair competition, which includes all activities against fair dealing and approved trade custom (Article 87). Examples are given in art 88 as follows:

(a) any activity which might create confusion in any way in respect of the business, product or activities of a competitor;

(b) false statements made in the course of business which may discredit the business, the product or the industrial or commercial activity of a competitor;

(c) giving false or misleading indications, either directly or indirectly, as to the origin of a product or service or the identity of the producer, manufacturer or trader.

Those affected by any activity amounting to unfair competition may initiate proceedings, and both civil and criminal remedies are available. In addition to the rules contained in Law 32/88, the rules provided by Law 3/1991 (*Competencia Desleal*) referred to in Chapter 2 should also be taken into account.

1.2.5 HARMONISATION OF EC LEGISLATION

Both the 1986 Law on Patents and the 1988 Law on Trade Marks have the aim of harmonising Spanish law with EC legislation. The 1986 Law introduced the patentability of chemical and pharmaceutical products, provided patent holders with some new remedies such as the possibility of applying for an injunction, and enacted some specific rules of evidence in patent proceedings.

Regarding trade marks and the EC Directive of 1988, the new Trade Mark Law introduced protection for the user of a trade mark, in addition to the rights acquired as the result of a trade mark registration. The rights of those owners of well known unregistered trade marks, as indicated under para 1.2.1, should also be remembered. The new law also tries to provide some legal remedies in respect of trade mark violations, including the cancellation of trade marks registered under the old law if they contravene the new law in any respect. Another important amendment introduced by the new law is the requirement that a trade mark must be used to be kept in force.

1.3 INDUSTRIAL MODELS AND DESIGNS (*MODELOS Y DIBUJOS INDUSTRIALES*)

The rules applicable to designs created for the industrial exploitation of a product, are those contained in the 1929 Industrial Property Law (*Estatuto de la Propiedad Industrial*). Article 182 defines an industrial model, to include any new three-dimensional design created for the manufacture of a product. Industrial designs registration applies to two-dimensional designs, these being lines and colours for ornamental purposes. The rights arising from registration last for ten years and may be renewable provided that fees are paid every five years to maintain them.

Registration is obtained by application through the Industrial Property Registry. For these purposes, it is required that there must be a new form susceptible of industrial exploitation. There are certain prohibitions from registration which include, *inter alia*, The Red Cross emblem, and national or foreign emblems (unless authorised) etc.

The application is made on an official form, to which the description of the model or design is appended. Numerous formal details are mentioned in the form which need to be complied with. After a preliminary review to verify that none of the prohibitions are applicable and that the required documentation has been attached, a notice is published in the Official Gazette. Third parties have a two month period in which to object before the Registrar to the application for registration, and the applicant has the right to reply to the objections within 15 days of the publication in the Official Gazette (*Boletin Oficial de la Propiedad Industrial*). After this, the Registrar decides whether to approve or reject the application. This decision must be published in the Official Gazette.

Both civil and criminal remedies in the courts are available to protect rights arising from registration against those exploiting the industrial model or design without the registered owner's authorisation. Injunctions, interim remedies and damages are also available through civil proceedings.

Spain is a party to various international Conventions, as for example the 1925 Hague Convention regulating International Filing of Industrial Models and Designs and the 1968 Locarno Agreement on Industrial Classification of Industrial Designs and Models.

1.4 LICENSING

1.4.1 PATENTS

The rules applicable to the licensing of patents in Spain are those of Law 18/86. Chapters 2 and 3 of Title VIII and Title IX provide detailed rules in connection with the licensing of patents.

As a guideline the following points should be noted:

(1) The licensing of patents may be exclusive or non-exclusive.
(2) Unless agreed to the contrary, the licensor must make available to the licensee the technical information required to exploit the invention. The licensee must adopt all the necessary measures to protect the secrecy of this information.
(3) Licence agreements must be registered at the Registry of Intellectual Properties.
(4) If the holder of a patent does not use his patent rights for a period of four years, the government may require that a licence be granted for exploitation of the patent (art 86 of Law 11/86). Any person may apply for the grant of this mandatory licence if without reason exploitation has not taken place or where the exploitation of the patent has been interrupted for more than three years. This mandatory licence is not exclusive, unless the public interest so requires.

1.4.2 TRADE MARKS

The licensing of trade marks is regulated by Law 32/1988, in particular by Chapter 3.

As a guideline the following may be indicated:

(1) Both the application for registration as well as a trade mark itself may be licensed in respect of all the products and services applicable or only in respect of part of them.
(2) The licence may be exclusive or non-exclusive.
(3) The licence agreement has to be registered at the Registry of Intellectual Property. The application for registration of licence agreements must comply with some specific legal requirements such as, for example, a clear identification of the registered owner of the trade mark and the licensee, and payment of fees. The applications are published in the Official Gazette of Industrial Property.

Decided cases also take into account EC law such as, for example, those provided by EC Regulations 2349/84 applicable to patent licensing agreements relating to block exemptions under Article 85.3 of the Treaty of Rome.

1.5 KNOW-HOW

There are no specific rules dealing with know-how agreements. The concept of know-how is usually understood as referring to a new technique or invention which is kept secret but with its use authorised by contract. The Supreme Court in a judgment of 24 October 1974 referred to know-how as knowledge or method which may have commercial or industrial significance. In addition, the decided cases have also considered as relevant the provisions of EC Regulation 556/89 dealing with the licensing of know-how.

In practice, it is possible to enter into a contract licensing know-how, as there is freedom of contract (see Chapter 5) in respect of commercial contracts; the applicable basic rules will be those of the Commercial Code, Commercial Practice and the Civil Code. Additional specific rules may also be relevant, such as for example those on transfer of technology (Royal Decree 1750/87). In any event, in addition to these rules, there will be some specific circumstances that may need to be taken into account, for example if the exploitation of any patent is involved or if competition rules need to be considered.

In general terms, a Spanish agreement licensing of know-how should contain the following clauses:

(a)   clear identification of the parties;
(b)   obligations of the parties should be clearly stated. The licensor, for example, must make available to the licensee the technical knowledge included together with the necessary assistance to put this to work. The licensee undertakes to effect payment in respect of the information received and also undertakes to keep secret the information provided by the licensor. The parties may also agree some indemnities, for example, the licensor may guarantee the result of the knowledge;
(c)   causes for termination of the agreement;
(d)   duration of the agreement;
(e)   confidentiality clauses;
(f)   law applicable and jurisdiction in the event of a dispute.

1.6   COPYRIGHT

1.6.1   INTRODUCTION

The rules relating to copyright are provided by Law 22/87 on Intellectual Property. In addition, Spain is a party to the Geneva Universal Convention on Authors' Rights of 1952 and a member of the 1986 Berne Union for the Protection of Literary and Artistic Works.

The law provides rules in respect of copyright, the rights of actors, musicians and other performers, sound recordings, audio-visual recordings, broadcasting and photographic work. Some of the provisions included in this law have been further implemented by numerous royal decrees on some specific matters.

1.6.2   COPYRIGHT ENTITLEMENTS

The Spanish Constitution includes in Article 2.1b, the right to literary, scientific and technical production and creation which needs to be recognised and protected.

The general rule is that a literary, artistic or scientific work create rights for its author and that there is no need for registration. If the author does decide to register his work he can do so at the Spanish Copyright Registry (*Registro de Propiedad*

Intelectual). Copyright protection is given to the author. It may also be granted to other persons such as, for example, co-authors and editors.

The rights granted to the author include moral rights and exploitation rights over his work. The first relates to the rights on whether his work should be published and in what manner, and the protection of his right to recognition as author of the work. Violation of these rights may entitle the author to claim compensation in damages. Exploitation rights will include the right to reproduce and distribute his work. As a general rule, exploitation rights will last for the life of the author plus a further 60 years after his death. Exploitation rights, unlike moral rights, may be assigned in writing to third parties.

In addition to the damages referred to, copyright holders may seek an injunction through civil proceedings. They may also start criminal proceedings with penalties ranging from fines to imprisonment according to the seriousness of the offence.

1.6.3 COMPUTER LAW

The 1987 Copyright Law grants protection in respect of computer programs, technical documentation and users' manual. It also provides that a computer program is patentable where it forms part of a product that is patentable, or has protection as a utility model (see 1.1.3).

2
COMPETITION LAW

2.1 INTRODUCTION

The Treaty of Rome which was signed on 25 March 1957 sets out in art 3 several desiderata for the purpose of achieving the Common Market objectives, one of these being the establishment of freedom of movement for goods, services, persons and capital between the member states and continued development and expansion of economic activities, including 'the institution of a system ensuring that competition in the Common Market is not distorted'. Further, competition is dealt with more specifically under arts 85 and 86. Community Law provides as a general principle that agreements between undertakings are prohibited as incompatible with the Common Market if such agreements may affect trade between member states and have as their object the prevention, restriction or distortion of competition within the Common Market, or the abuse by one of the parties of a dominant position. Those carrying out economic activities therefore need to ensure that they remain within the boundaries of both European and domestic competition Law. Spain joined the European Community from January 1986 and European competition law now forms part of its domestic law.

2.2 EC COMPETITION LAW

As indicated above, arts 85 and 86 of the Treaty of Rome deal with agreements between parties which may affect trade between member states.

2.2.1 ARTICLE 85

Article 85(1) states the broad prohibition in respect of those 'agreements between undertakings, decisions by associations of undertakings and concerted practices which may affect trade

between member states and which have as their object or effect
the prevention, restriction or distortion of competition within
the Common Market'. By way of illustration, five particular types
of agreements are listed as prohibited, including, those agreements which directly or indirectly fix purchase or selling prices or
any trading conditions; and agreements which share markets or
sources of supply.

Article 85(2) declares that agreements or decisions prohibited by art 85(1) shall be automatically void.

2.2.2 EXCEPTIONS

Notice of Agreements of Minor Importance

In accordance with the Commission's Notice of Agreements
of Minor Importance (September 1986), agreements between
small or medium sized companies are unlikely to fall within the
prohibitions stated by art 85(1). Accordingly, for example, an
agreement will be deemed to have no effect on trade or
competition between member states where the goods or services
which are the subject of the agreement represent not more than 5
per cent of the total market for those goods or services and where
the aggregate turnover of the undertakings involved does not
exceed ECU 200m. Complications may arise as to the calculation
of the relevant 5 per cent, as this depends on the definition of the
relevant market. Those who are party to an agreement falling
within this exception should review their position from time to
time and check, for example, if the growth of their businesses still
allows them to be excepted.

Note that the above are only guidelines, as the Commission
would not allow blatantly restrictive agreements, for example,
even if these agreements are between parties with market share
and turnover below the limits.

Article 85(3)

Further, the European Commission has the power to grant
(or refuse) exemption if the parties have notified the Commission
for this purpose. Article 85(3) provides some exceptions to the
prohibitions under art 85(1), for those agreements, decisions or
concerted practice(s) which contribute 'to improving the production or distribution of goods or to promoting technical or
economic progress while allowing the consumers a fair share of
the resulting benefit', provided that they do not impose restric-

tions which are not necessary for achieving these objectives and also that they do not provide the possibility 'of eliminating competition in respect of a substantial part of the products in question'. An illustration of the above exception was a joint venture between Olivetti and Canon, which was investigated by the Commission during December 1986; it was concluded that in this case the economic and technological advantages for the Common Market outweighed the restrictions caused.

2.2.3 ARTICLE 86

This provision prohibits 'any abuse, by one or more undertaking, of a dominant position within the Common Market'. Article 86 does not give a definition but instead lists four particular activities to illustrate the general prohibition, such as for example the fact of imposing directly or indirectly unfair selling prices or unfair trading conditions. Article 86 does not provide for any exemption to be granted, and it has thus been for the Commission to examine complaints and decide upon them. In many cases, these decisions have been appealed to the European Court which has the power to modify or overrule the Commission's decisions.

2.2.4 REGULATION 17

The above regulation, which deals with the application of arts 85 and 86, came into force in March 1962. It contains special provisions regarding the notification of agreements, decisions and concerted practices of the kind described in art 85(1) and in respect of which the parties seek application of art 85(3), and also provides the grounds for further exceptions under art 4(2) of the Regulations. In addition to the notification procedure, it also deals with enforcement, that is fines against those parties in breach of their obligations under arts 85(1) or 86, or rules provided by this Regulation.

Parties to an agreement should check that their activities comply with the rules provided by general European competition law, and also with relevant domestic laws. In the case of Spain, particular attention should be given to the provisions under the Competition Protection Law (*Ley de Defensa de la Competencia*) of 1989 and a further law, the Unfair Competition Law (*Ley de Competencia Desleal*) of 1991.

2.3 SPANISH COMPETITION LAW

2.3.1 LAW 16 OF 17 JULY 1989 — COMPETITION PROTECTION LAW (*DEFENSA DE LA COMPETENCIA*)

Article 38 of the Spanish Constitution states that the public authorities shall guarantee and protect the exercise of free enterprise and safeguard productivity in accordance with the demands of the economy. This provision together with European competition rules are the main sources of inspiration for the drafters of Law 16/89.

This law deals with the following:
* prohibited practices;
* mergers and acquisitions; and
* state subsidies.

Competition in terms of prohibited practices and exemptions is dealt with by Title I of the law.

Prohibitions

Article 1 of the law provides a general prohibition, and lists some specific activities. It prohibits any agreement, decision, collective proposal or concerted practice which is intended, results or is likely to impede, restrict or distort competition in the national market or part of it. Among these prohibited practices the following are specifically mentioned:

(a) price fixing (direct or indirect);
(b) fixing of commercial or service terms;
(c) restricting or controlling production, distribution, technical development or investment;
(d) the allocation of the market or sources of supply.

Agreements relating to prohibited activities are automatically void unless they fall within any of the available exceptions in this law.

Abuse of dominant position

Article 6 prohibits any abuse of a dominant position within the national market or in a part of it by one or more companies. This general prohibition is complemented by a list of activities which will be deemed to be such an abuse. These may consist in:

(a) directly or indirectly imposing unfair prices or commercial or service conditions;

(b) limiting production or distribution to companies or consumers;

(c) unjustifiably refusing to satisfy demands for goods or services;

(d) imposing unequal conditions for equivalent transactions or services resulting in disadvantages for some competitors;

(e) entering into agreements on condition that other extra obligations are undertaken which are not related to the agreements in accordance with commercial custom.

Exemptions

Article 3 provides the grounds for exemptions from those prohibtions of art 1. These exemptions may be granted by the Court for Protection of Competition (*Tribunal de Defensa de la Competencia*). This is the case, for example, when it is found that an agreement, decision or practice contributes to improving the production, distribution of services and goods or promotes technical or economic progress, provided that these allow the consumers to have a fair share of the benefits and, in addition, do not impose 'restrictions' on the parties involved, unless these are indispensable for these objectives and do not result in the possibility of eliminating competition in respect of a substantial part of the goods or services in question. Under art 3.2, the Court may grant other exemptions, taking into account the general economic situation and public interest. Among the activities which may fall within this heading the Court may consider, *inter alia*, the following:

(a) those activities which aim to defend or promote exports, in accordance with the obligations arising from treaties signed by Spain;

(b) those agreements, decisions and practices which are deemed to be too weak to have an appreciable effect on competition.

2.3.2 COMPETITION PROTECTION AND SANCTIONS

The Administrative Court

The Court for the Protection of Competition (*Tribunal de Defensa de la Competencia*) is given exclusive jurisdiction to deal with matters arising under the 1989 Law. There is the right of appeal from its decisions to the Supreme Court.

Sanctions

The Court may impose sanctions, including fines, upon those in breach of the provisions of the 1989 Law. In the case of corporations, in addition to the fines imposed on them, the Court may also impose a fine upon their legal representatives, or directors who have voted in favour of the resolution in breach of the rules of the 1989 law. At the time of writing, fines may be applied for up to an amount of 150,000,000 Ptas. This amount may be increased for up to 10 per cent of the sales as recorded in the accounting period prior to the Court decision.

In addition to financial penalties, the Court can issue injunctions (*medidas cautelares*) for the practices being investigated to cease in order to prevent their harmful effects.

Other administrative bodies

The 1989 Law has created two bodies to protect competition and the interests of consumers. These are:

- the Bureau for the Protection of Competition (*Servicio de Defensa de la Competencia*) (arts 30 *et seq*). Its functions, include ensuring that the decisions of the Court are executed; and investigations relating to the application of competition law;

- the Registry of Restrictive Practices (*Registro de Defensa de la Competencia*) (art 35). This Registry, which is open to the public, includes among its records the decisions, recommendations or practices authorised by the Court, as well as those prohibited totally or in part.

Law 16/89 has recently been further implemented by a Decree of 11 September 1992 enacting some procedural rules for the application of Law 16. It provides for voluntary notices to be given by companies planning to acquire or take control of other companies. This notice, on an official form, is served on the authorities of the *Servicio de Defensa de la Competencia*. The authorities will refer to the Court (*Tribunal de Defensa de la Competencia*) those cases which they consider to be an obstacle to free competition within the market. If the Court is not notified within one month from service of the voluntary notice by the parties, it can be concluded that the authorities have no objections to the particular transaction. The authorities are granted powers to request additional information from those planning to acquire or take control of some companies. The authorities' decisions must be notified to the parties, duly registered in the Registry and then published in the Official Gazette (*Boletin Oficial del Estado*).

The Decree also enacts procedural rules for the Special Court Dealing with Competition (*Tribunal de Defensa de la Competencia*).

2.3.3 LAW 3/1991 ON UNFAIR COMPETITION (*LEY DE COMPETENCIA DESLEAL*)

The aim of this Law is to protect the interest of businessmen and consumers. It enacts a general prohibition in art 5 by stating that all activities not in good faith are deemed to be unfair, with specific prohibitions such as the carrying out of activities causing confusion, exploiting the good reputation of others, breach of confidentiality etc. A claim may be brought by any person who has suffered or is likely to suffer damage as the result of the occurrence of an unfair act. This reflects the interest of the law in protecting the consumer. Proceedings to enforce the provisions of this law are governed by the rules applicable to civil proceedings for minor claims (*Juicio de Menor Cuantia*).

3
BUSINESS ORGANISATION

3.1 PARTNERSHIPS AND SOLE TRADERS

3.1.1 SOLE TRADERS

(i) *Introduction*: During the Middle Ages a new class of professionals engaged in mercantile life emerged in Spain. Their practices gradually became recognised as law which regulated their professional activities. The development of the trading centres, usually ports, led to the creation of specialised tribunals dealing with mercantile matters (*consulados*). In time, the law was developed to cope with the new practices. This briefly is the background to the development of the laws dealing with the needs of the mercantile community, among them the concept of the commercial contract. The law of the merchants was reflected in Spain in the late 19th century through the Commercial Code.

(ii) *Applicable provisions*: The activities of sole traders are generally regulated by the Commercial Code. Article 1 of the Commercial Code defines commercial persons as:

   (a) those who have legal capacity to engage in commerce and exercise it as their profession; and

   (b) those commercial or industrial corporations set up in accordance with the provisions of the Commercial Code.

The Commercial Code therefore establishes the criteria for those who are able to act as traders. For individuals, the requirements as to their capacity is that they have to be of full age (over 18) and are not disqualified from dealing with their assets. A sole trader may register in the Commercial Registry. If he does not, he cannot claim benefit of some important protection, such as the registration of documents and their resulting evidential value. Traders dealing with shipping activities are obliged to register. The Commercial Registry keeps records of sole traders including records of powers of attorney, matrimonial regime, commercial name etc.

Sole traders must keep some accounts of their activities. The Commercial Registry keeps a record of the books, and certifies the various records as stated in such books.

3.1.2 PARTNERSHIPS

Small investors and family businesses have kept partnerships alive.

(i) *Liability*: Partners have an unlimited joint and several liability for partnership debts and obligations.

(ii) *Legislation*: Commercial partnerships are regulated by the Commercial Code. A partnership can also be created under the Civil Code, and these will normally be subject to the rules of insolvency. In accordance with the rule of the Civil Code (art 35) both types of partnerships have legal personality.

Article 119 of the Commercial Code deals with the formation of general partnerships in Spain.

(1) Partnerships, which are based on a contractual agreement, need a notarised deed;

(2) The deed must be registered at the Commercial Register;

(3) In addition, any deeds amending the original agreement must also be registered.

Such a deed should contain all the special terms and conditions agreed between the parties and also the main object of the partnership, the full details of each of the partners, particulars of the partners who are responsible for the management (if it is agreed that one or only some of them will be in charge of this), the capital contributed by each partner and the duration of the partnership (art 125 of the Commercial Code).

(iii) *Partners' Rights*: Partnerships may operate under the name of all the parties or only some of them, but in the latter case the words 'and company' (*y compañia*) must be stated. As previously stated, partners have an unlimited joint and several liability for partnership debts and obligations even if they do not deal directly with administration of the partnership. On the other hand, partners have the right to verify the administration and accounts and have access to all books and records of the company. As to the distribution of profits and losses, these are normally agreed in the contract. If this is not the case, these are shared in proportion to the capital contribution of each partner.

3.1.3   LIMITED PARTNERSHIPS

Sociedad en Comandita

(i)   *Partners*: Article 122 of the Commercial Code lists commercial companies and includes limited partnerships (*sociedad en comandita*). In such a partnership there are two kinds of partners, general partners (*socios colectivos*); and limited partners (*socios comanditarios*). Their liabilities are different. In the former case, the partners are personally liable for all the debts of the partnerships, and in the latter case their liability is limited to their investment in the partnership.

(ii)   *Incorporation*: Article 145 of the Commercial Code provides that the deed of incorporation should contain the same information as that required for a general partnership. The regulations applicable to the registration of this type of partnership state that it is also necessary to distinguish between those partners who are to be the general partners (*socios colectivos*) and those who are limited partners (*socios comanditarios*).

(iii)   *Management*: A *sociedad en comandita* operates under the name of the general partners (or of only one of them plus the words 'and company'), and in any event the words *sociedad en comandita* should always be included. The rights and obligations of the general partners are the same as those in a general partnership, except that the limited partners are only liable in equal proportion to their capital contributions and up the limit of these. An important exception to this rule is that of the limited partner whose name appears in the name of the partnership: he has unlimited liability.

(iv)   *Sociedad en comandita por acciones*: Another possibility of limited partnership is offered by a limited partnership with shares (*sociedad en comandita por acciones*). In this case, the contribution of limited partners is represented by shares (*acciones*). It is a legal requirement that there should be at least one partner who will have unlimited liability. The name of the company should indicate the name of the general partner(s) plus the words *sociedad en comandita por acciones* or 'S, Com. por A'. Limited partnerships with shares are regulated by the rules of the Commercial Code and also by some of the rules of law applicable to one of the limited companies (*Sociedad Anonima*).

As with the rest of partnerships, partners remain important as individuals, for example, in the case of the dissolution of the firm. Article 157 of the Commercial Code states that this type of firm is dissolved in the event of the death of the general manager(s) or their bankruptcy or disability. Further, the dismissal or appointment of a general manager requires the amendment of the articles of association (*estatutos Sociales*) by unanimous consent of all the partners.

3.2 LIMITED LIABILITY COMPANIES

3.2.1 SOCIEDAD ANONIMA (SA)

This is one of the most popular options for many businesses, including joint ventures. The *sociedad anonima* is a company with a capital divided into shares. The shareholders are liable up to the extent of their capital investment. This type of company is classified in the Commercial Code as commercial. The law dealing with these sort of companies has been amended to adapt to Spanish business legislation. The applicable law is known as *Ley de las Sociedades Anonimas*.

3.2.2 SOCIEDAD LIMITADA (SL)

This type of company is also classified in the Commercial Code as a commercial company. It also has a share capital, but interests in the capital are not called shares as in the case of a SA (*acciones*). The share capital is divided into '*participaciones*'. This type of company is normally associated only with small businesses. However, the new rules applicable to the SA, with a minimum share capital of 10 million pesetas, have made this type of company a popular alternative for companies previously existing in the form of an SA, and many SAs have become SLs.

An important difference between the SL type of company and the SA company is the fact that shares in the latter are normally freely transferrable, whereas the *participaciones* are affected by special restrictions (see 3.4.3). These companies are regulated by the provisions of a special law, *Ley Sobre Regimen Juridico de las Sociedades de Responsabilidad Limitada*.

3.3 INCORPORATION OF LIMITED COMPANIES

3.3.1 INTRODUCTION

For both SAs and SLs there are some general requirements in connection with their incorporation. As a preliminary matter it is necessary to deal with the company name. The normal practice is to reserve more than one name in case the preferred choice is not available. A trade certificate will be issued in each case, to ensure that there will be no other Spanish company with the same name. The whole procedure should take about 10–15 days. General requirements would also include the deed of incorporation and registration in the Commercial Registry (*Registro Mercantil*). Before registration is effected a tax of 1 per cent on the share capital has to be paid (*impuesto Sobre Transmisiones Patrimoniales*).

As part of the procedure of incorporation of these companies, a tax number (*NIF–Numero de Identificacion Fiscal*) must be obtained, and also a special licence relating to the type of the activity that the company will carry out (*Licencia Fiscal*).

3.3.2 DEED OF INCORPORATION

(i) *Sociedad Anonima*: Article 8 of the law on SAs states the requirements of the deed of incorporation. It must contain, *inter alia*:

    (a) particulars of the original shareholders (not less than three);

    (b) particulars of contributions of each shareholder; and

    (c) particulars of those who will manage and represent the company.

The deed of incorporation should also include the articles of association (*Estatutos*). Article 9 of the law on SAs prescribes in detail all the information that should be included in the articles of association, which must set out, for example, the date of commencement of operation, the main object of the company, the registered office, the accounting date, the procedure for shareholders meetings, the board of directors, etc.

(ii)   *Sociedad Limitada*: Similarly, the law on SLs (art 7) also deals in detail with the information which must be included in the deed of incorporation. This deed of incorporation must include *inter alia*:

    (a)   details of each of the members;
    (b)   the company name;
    (c)   the object of the company;
    (d)   the registered office;
    (e)   share capital and contributions of each member;
    (f)   duration of the company;
    (g)   procedure for shareholders' meetings.

    Under Spanish law, both in the case of a *Sociedad Anonima* and a *Sociedad Limitada*, more than one founding member is required for SAs, three founding members, and for SLs two founding members. However, in the event that any of these companies become single member companies, the company does not have to dissolve and may continue with one member who has limited liability. This interpretation has been reflected in case law. Furthermore, the General Directorate of Registries and Notaries (*Direccion General de los Registros y del Notariado*) issued a decision in 1990 (21 June 1990) confirming the validity of a limited company which has only one remaining member after been duly incorporated.

(iii)   *Deed of Incorporation of a Sociedad Anonima (SA)*: As a guideline, a deed of incorporation, which needs to be executed before a notary public, may be set up by taking the following steps:

    (1)   The parties appear before the notary public identifying themselves and stating the capacity in which they are acting. If they are acting by virtue of a power of attorney, this document will be requested by the Notary. Where the power of attorney was granted in another country, eg in England, it must be authenticated by a notary and legalised with the Hague Apostille Seal.

    (2)   Details of the share capital of the company must be

given in the deed—in the case of an SA a minimum capital of 10,000,000 pesetas. The deed should also contain particulars of the shareholders and the shares acquired.

(3) Appointment of directors: The deed will state, for example, 'the following persons herein mentioned are appointed directors of the company for the period of [5] years. These appointments are to be considered as made in a general meeting'. This should be followed by particulars of the directors being appointed.

(4) The deed will also contain some other clauses and declarations, such as for example: 'the persons appearing declare that there is no other company of the same name in existence, and they herewith produce a certificate to this effect issued by the Commercial Registry'. The deed is signed by the persons appearing and the public notary will certify the content of the deed.

(iv) *Articles of Association*: So far as the articles of association of the company are concerned, these must include the following:

(a) the name of the company and the statement that the company will be regulated by the articles of association and by the relevant legislation in force;

(b) the objects of the company;

(c) duration of the company and starting date of its activities. To this effect the clause may read as follows:
'The company is incorporated for a period of . . . (or for an indefinite period) and its activities shall commence . . .';

(d) details of the registered office;

(e) a statement of the share capital of the company;

(f) details of the shares of the company. This clause may read:
'The shares shall be represented by certificates numbered . . .';

(g) procedure for the transfer of shares. This could include, for example, advance notice to be given to the board of directors, and the period of time for receiving notification of those intending to acquire the shares offered. This clause may include, a provision such as the following:

'Any shareholder who intends to transfer his shares shall notify his intentions clearly to the board of directors. The board of directors will give notice to the rest of the shareholders. Both notices shall contain the number of shares which are to be transferred, the person who intends to be the transferee, the price and the conditions agreed. The shareholders or shareholders interested in the shares shall notify the company within a period of . . . .

If none of the shareholders intend to acquire the shares offered, the company may acquire these shares within the period of . . . days. If neither the shareholder nor the company shall be interested in the shares and the board authorises the transfer, this may be effected within a two month period';

(h)   details of meetings of the company, for example:

an ordinary general meeting must be held, after being duly notified, within the first six months of each financial year to consider and approve, if appropriate, the accounts and any resolutions in this connection. All the other meetings shall be considered extraordinary. The board shall convene such a meeting . . .;

(i)   details of notices of the meetings;

(j)   details of quorums required for the meetings;

(k)   details of the formalities in connection with any proxy, for example a clause stating that

any shareholder may appoint another person, or maybe another shareholder as his proxy. The instrument appointing a proxy must be executed in writing for each individual meeting . . .;

(l)   details of procedures at the meetings, for example:

The proceedings of general meetings shall be recorded in minutes. The minutes shall be signed by the secretary and counter-signed by the chairman or the vice chairman . . .;

(m) details of the administration and representation of the company, eg the minimum and maximum number of directors and the duration of their appointments. It will also state whether directors may be entitled to receive any payment, and the procedure for filling any vacancies among the number of directors;

(n) procedure relating to meetings of the board of directors, including the quorum for such meetings;

(o) powers of the directors. This clause may state, for example:

> The directors have the powers to represent the company including all those activities within the objects of the company as hereto described, by way of example the following: . . .;

(p) other powers of the board of directors such as the power to appoint one or more of its members as managing directors and to create committees of the board to exercise some specific powers;

(q) details of the annual accounts for example: 'The fiscal year begins on the 1 January each year and shall end on 31 December of the same year';

(r) obligations of the directors in respect of the annual accounts of the company, for example:

> 'The directors shall submit at the end of the fiscal year the annual accounts of the company duly signed within a period of three months. The annual accounts shall comprise. . . .'

The articles of association will naturally take account of the specific requirements of the shareholders involved and this will be reflected in the quorums decided and the composition of the board of directors, taking into account the minimum legal requirements.

3.3.3 REGISTRATION OF THE COMPANY

Commercial companies acquire legal personality only after being duly registered at the Commercial Registry. In the case of an SA it is necessary for at least 25 per cent of the authorised share capital to be paid up. An SA must register within two months of the date on which the deed of incorporation was executed. Share capital may be fully subscribed; alternatively, the minimum 25 per cent may be paid and the rest may then be offered to the public (*fundacion sucesiva*). Spanish law has no concept of authorised but unissued shares.

An SL must have a minimum authorised share capital of 500,000 pesetas fully paid up on incorporation and therefore before registration.

3.4   SHARES

3.4.1   INTRODUCTION

The share capital of the SA and the capital of an SL are divided into parts. Both the *acciones* of the former and the *participaciones* (see 3.1.3 and 3.2.2 above) of the latter give the holders their respective rights as members of the company.

3.4.2   TYPES OF SHARES

(i)   *Sociedad Anonima*: There may be different classes of shares, namely ordinary and preference shares. An interesting feature of recent changes to Spanish company law affecting the SA is the fact that shares without voting rights can also be issued. These shares are entitled to preferential benefits, for example in connection with the distribution of dividends.

Shares may be either registered (*nominativas*) or bearer shares (*al portador*). All shares are issued from a book *libro talonario* and the law specifies the minimum details which have to be recorded (art 53, Law on SA), such as the type of share, value and number etc.

(ii)   *Sociedad Limitada*: SL *participaciones* are, like SA shares indivisible, but they are all of the same class; and it is not possible to have preference shares.

3.4.3   TRANSFER OF SHARES

(i)   *Sociedad Anonima*: The general rule is that shares in an SA are transferable, although some restrictions may be imposed, perhaps in the articles of association (*Estatutos*), on the transfer of registered shares.

Spanish company law does not permit restrictions which totally prohibit transferability (art 63.2, Law on SA). Transfer of bearer shares takes place upon delivery. Transfers of registered shares may be effected by endorsement in accordance with the rules of the Exchange and Cheque Law (*Ley Cambiaria y del Cheque*), in particular arts 15, 16, 19 and 20. Transfers have to be registered in the share register (*Libro Registro*).

(ii) *Sociedad Limitada: Participaciones* are normally transferred to other members of the company, and must be offered to the other shareholders first of all. They may not be traded in the stock market as in the case of some SA companies. However, as in the case of shares in an SA, pledges and other charges may be created on them. Transfers do not need to be registered in the Commercial Registry.

3.5 CAPITAL

3.5.1 MINIMUM CAPITAL REQUIREMENTS

(i) *Sociedad Anonima*: A minimum authorised share capital of 10 million pesetas is required with at least 25 per cent of the authorised share capital paid up at the time of the incorporation.

(ii) *Sociedad Limitada*: The minimum authorised share capital is 500,000 pesetas which needs to be fully paid up on incorporation. This means that promoters cannot offer these to the public as in the case of 'successive' incorporation (*fundacion sucesiva*): see 3.3.3.

3.5.2 PAYMENT FOR SHARES IN CASH

Cash payments must be made in pesetas. If payment is made in foreign currency it would be necessary to determine the amount equivalent in pesetas at the time that the shares are subscribed. This applies to both the *Sociedad Anonima* and *Sociedad Limitada*.

3.5.3 PAYMENTS IN KIND

The Spanish Company Law provisions applicable to a SA

state that contributions in kind need to be valued by one or more experts appointed by the Commercial Register. The rules of the Civil Code on title are applicable in the event of payments consisting of property and the rules of the Commercial Code are applicable in connection with transfer of risk. In any event, the relevant documentation should be submitted to the public notary dealing with the deed of incorporation (or increase of capital).

3.5.4 PURCHASE BY THE COMPANY OF ITS SHARES

(i) *Sociedad Anonima*: These companies generally are not allowed to subscribe to their own shares, or to those of a holding company, but the law regulates the requirements for those exceptional circumstances when it is permitted. For example, an authorisation must be granted at a shareholders' meeting, and must contain details of the maximum number of shares, minimum and maximum price of shares and the duration of the authorisation, which in any event may not exceed 18 months.

(ii) *Sociedad Limitada*: A company may acquire a member's interest in the company through the general procedure established for transfers (see 3.4.3). Written notice must be given to the directors, who will give notice within 15 days to the existing members. In the event that no member is interested (or does not exercise his option rights within 30 days) then the company may exercise its rights to acquire.

3.5.5 INCREASE AND REDUCTION OF CAPITAL

(i) *Sociedad Anonima*: As will be explained in 3.6.4, strict compliance with the special rules governing this type of shareholders' resolution is required for their validity. In addition, it should be borne in mind that all amendments to the articles of association must be contained in a deed executed before a public notary and filed with the Commercial Register. An increase of capital may be the result, for example, of cash payments, payments in kind, conversion of debt into equity leading to the issue of shares etc. In the case of a reduction of capital, in addition to the protective provisions for shareholders, creditors are generally given a one month period within which to object.

(ii) *Sociedad Limitada*: A decision to increase or reduce capital requires strict observance of the prescribed procedure, including a notarised deed duly registered at the Commercial Register and the necessary quorum, which in the case of a first meeting will require a majority of the members representing at least two-thirds of the capital, and in the case of an adjourned meeting those representing two-thirds of the capital will suffice.

3.6 SHAREHOLDERS' MEETINGS

3.6.1 INTRODUCTION

The right to attend and vote at shareholders' meetings is one of the basic rights of shareholders (except as to non-voting shares with respect to the right to vote). The members pass resolutions in accordance with the procedures prescribed by law and by the articles of association.

3.6.2 PROCEDURAL REQUIREMENTS

Spanish company law lays down minimum requirements as to, for example the quorum for passing some important resolutions such as for dissolution of the company. The shareholders may decide to increase their required quorums.

(i) *Sociedad Anonima*: SA shareholders' meetings need to comply with notice formalities (*Convocatoria*), unless it is a special type of meeting called 'universal'. The notice of the meeting must state:
   (a) the date of the meeting;
   (b) the agenda;
   (c) the date of a second meeting if no quorum is reached at the first meeting.

All resolutions must be in writing and some of them need to be duly notarised and registered (see 3.6.4 below).

(ii) *Sociedad Limitada*: SL procedure requirements are normally simpler than in the case of an SA, for example a meeting is not always required to adopt resolutions. This rule has some exceptions, for example if the company has more than 15 members. Generally, the members will choose the procedure that they want to follow, except where the law prescribes some mandatory requirements, for example as to the minimum quorum required to pass resolutions for increasing or reducing the share capital of the company.

3.6.3   RIGHTS OF THE SHAREHOLDERS AT THE MEETINGS

(i)   *Sociedad Anonima*: The shareholders of a SA company may act through meetings which may be ordinary (ie for the approval of the accounts), extraordinary, or 'universal'. Ordinary meetings must be called by the directors during the first six months of each financial year. Extraordinary meetings may be called at any time, either at initiative of the directors or by request of shareholders who must represent at least 5 per cent of paid-up capital. A universal meeting may take place only when all the shareholders are present and agree to hold a meeting. Shareholders may appoint a proxy to represent them at any specific meetings. Shareholders representing at least 1 per cent of the share capital may request that a notary attend a particular meeting to notarise the resolutions passed.

(ii) *Sociedad Limitada*: The provisions of the law on SLs allow for voluntary meetings which are called by the directors in accordance with the articles of association of the company, and also meetings which are mandatory if they are requested by members holding at least one-quarter of the capital. A meeting may also be called if all members are present and agree to hold a meeting. In this case there is no need for notices.

      As in the case of the SA, the general rule is that shareholders may appoint in writing a person as a proxy to represent them at any specified meeting.

3.6.4   SHAREHOLDERS' RESOLUTIONS

(i)   *Sociedad Anonima*: Quorum requirements differ according to whether it is the first meeting or an adjournment. In the first case, a quorum of members with 25 per cent of paid-up capital is required. However, the law prescribes higher quorums in some instances, for example amendment to articles of association or an increase or decrease of capital. For these special events a quorum of 50 per cent of paid-up capital is required at the first meeting and 25 per cent on any adjourment. It must be stated however, that the law requires a two-thirds majority for resolutions at meetings attended by members holding less than 50 per cent of paid-up capital.

(ii) *Sociedad Limitada*: The general rule is that resolutions are passed by a majority of members, unless otherwise agreed by them. However, there are restrictions in the case of some essential events affecting the company such as:

(a) increasing or reducing the capital;
(b) extending the duration of the company;
(c) merger or transformation of the company;
(d) amendment of the deed of incorporation.

In the above circumstances, resolutions need to be passed by a majority of members representing at least two-thirds of the capital at a first meeting, and on an adjournment by any number of the members representing two-thirds of the capital. In addition the law requires that these changes be incorporated in a deed which must be registered at the Commercial Registry.

3.6.5 CHALLENGING RESOLUTIONS

The general rule is that shareholders of a SA or SL are bound by resolutions passed at a shareholders meeting. However, SA and SL resolutions may be challenged on the grounds that they are in breach of the law or the articles of association, or are against the interest of the company for the benefit of one or more shareholders or a third party. In the first case, resolutions are void and in the latter voidable, and claims against the company must be made within 40 days from the date of the approval of the resolution, or from its publication in the event that this was registered with the Commercial Registry.

Actions against the company in respect of void resolutions are barred after a year. However, this limitation does not apply if a resolution is against law and order. Challenges to a void resolution may be made by a shareholder, directors or by any interested third party. A claim against a voidable resolution, on the other hand, may be made only by those shareholders who did not attend the meeting or who voted against. Directors of the company are also entitled to lodge a challenge.

3.7 MANAGEMENT OF THE COMPANY AND SUPERVISION OF MANAGEMENT

3.7.1 APPOINTMENT AND DISMISSAL OF DIRECTORS

(i) *Sociedad Anonima*: The shareholders elect the directors (*administradores*), who may be an individual or a company. They need not be shareholders in the company, unless this has been stated in the articles of association. The appointment of directors is effective as from the date of acceptance and should be registered within the next ten days at the Commercial Registry. Directors are elected for a maximum period of five years, but re-election is possible. Directors who become disqualified eg by bankruptcy, may be dismissed immediately. The general rule is that directors may be dismissed at any time.

(ii) *Sociedad Limitada*: Directors of an SL are generally subject to the same rules as those of an SA. The law on SLs requires directors to be appointed by a majority of members and serve for the period indicated in the deed of incorporation. Normally they may also be dismissed at any time, by a simple majority of shareholders, unless their appointment is stated in the deed of incorporation. In that case, the quorum for amendments of deeds will be applicable (see above 3.6.4).

3.7.2 DUTIES AND AUTHORITY OF THE BOARD OF DIRECTORS

(i) *Sociedad Anonima*: (a) Board of Directors—An SA may have a sole director (*administrador unico*) or a board of directors (*Consejo de Administracion*). The administration of the company may be entrusted to a general manager(s) (*director general*), who is an officer of the company, or to a managing director (*consejero delegado*), who is a member of the board, or two or more of the directors.

(b) Powers of Directors—Directors are entrusted with management powers and powers of representation. The former are normally contained in the articles of association and the latter depend largely on the main objects of the company. However, the company will still be liable to third parties who acted in good faith in connection with operations not included within the objects of the company.

(ii) *Sociedad Limitada*: One or more directors may be entrusted with the powers of administration and representation of the company. In general terms, the rules for an SA will be applicable to these directors as well, although there are some specific restrictions on their activities. Article 12 of the Law on SLs states that the directors are precluded from engaging on their own account in the same type of business as that of the company. The powers of the directors will be contained in a deed executed before a public notary and duly registered at the Commercial Registry.

3.8 ANNUAL ACCOUNTS

The financial year begins on 1 January and ends on 31 December. Directors have to ensure that company accounts are prepared and submitted duly signed by all of them. These accounts will comprise a balance sheet, profit and loss account and a report. SA companies may be required to have their accounts reviewed by an independent auditor. Some companies are exempt from this requirement, for example, companies with less than 50 employees and assets totalling less than 230 million pesetas.

Accounting rules for SLs are the same as those for an SA (art 26, Law on SLs). Minority shareholders are protected and they may request the appointment of an independent auditor.

3.9 DISSOLUTION AND LIQUIDATION

3.9.1 DISSOLUTION

A company is dissolved at the end of the period agreed by members, or in other cases as prescribed by law for both SAs and SLs. The following are some of the causes for dissolution:

(a) merger or hive down of the company;
(b) impossibility of carrying out the objects of the company;
(c) insolvency of the company.

A resolution must be passed by the shareholders, which must comply with the prescribed formalities (see 3.6.4). It should also be registered in the Commercial Registry and duly published in the Official Gazette plus one other major newspaper in the area of the registered office.

3.9.2   LIQUIDATION

After the dissolution of the company, the liquidation procedure takes over. The liquidators continue with the final operations of the company, exercising all powers of management through this period. Their activities and responsibilities are regulated in detail by the Law on SAs. The aim of the liquidators is to determine the net worth of the company. After payment to creditors any balance will be divided among the members taking into account the articles of association. Liquidators are accountable to the shareholders and the creditors. Their final accounts need to be approved by the shareholders and then published in the Official Gazette and one other newspaper of major circulation in the area of the company's registered office.

4

MERGERS AND ACQUISITIONS

4.1 APPLICABLE RULES

(i) *Company Law*: The Law on *Sociedades Anonimas* (see 3.4.3) considers in art 233.1 two kinds of mergers:

    (a) agreements between any two companies which agree to merge creating a new company (*fusion*);

    (b) the takeover of one or more companies by an existing SA.

    The merger of a limited company is dealt with by the Law on *Sociedades Anonimas* as to the procedure and formalities. Mergers, are permitted between a *Sociedad Anonima* and other types of companies as will be explained below. In the event of a merger of other types of companies and partnerships, and where no SA is involved, the provisions dealing with any mergers or changes will be applicable.

(ii) *Competition Law*: In addition the 1989 Competition Protection Law (*Defensa de la Competencia*) should be taken into account as, in general, significant mergers or acquisitions must be recorded in a special register, the *Registro de Defensa de la Competencia* (see 2.3.2).

(iii) *Community Rules*: Community rules in respect of the Directives adopted in the field of direct taxation will have to be taken into account, and it is expected that new legislation will reflex tax harmonisation with EC rules, these have been only partially incorporated into the Spanish legal system.

    Regarding company mergers concerning companies of different member states (Directive No 90/434/EC), there is at present a draft tax law which envisages that mergers should be effected as neutrally as possible, so that companies may be able to merge without having to depend on the decision of the state authorities so far as tax benefits are concerned.

4.2 LEGAL FORMALITIES

4.2.1 INITIAL REPORTS

(i) A report must be prepared and signed by the company directors of each of the merging companies. If any signature is missing the cause should be duly stated in the document. The report must then be approved by a general meeting of each of the companies within a period of six months of its date.

The report must contain some minimum information, including the following:

(a) name and registered offices of the merging companies, and those of the proposed new company if applicable, together with the companies' registration details;

(b) details of share exchanges and any cash payments to shareholders if applicable;

(c) details of the procedure applicable for share exchanges, including the date as from which the new shares will have the right to receive profits;

(d) date from which the transactions of the companies which will cease are to be deemed as being carried out by the company receiving the capital, for accounting purposes;

(e) any rights or special benefits, to be granted in the new (or absorbing) company to those shareholders having preferential rights;

(f) any benefits or rights which will be granted to independent experts taking part in the merger.

(ii) The companies' reports are submitted for the consideration of experts appointed by the Commercial Registry, who will produce separate reports (or only one if so requested). The experts must state if the share capital of those companies which are going to cease is at least equal to that of the new company or to the increase of capital in the event that one company is taking over the other.

(iii) In addition, the directors of each of the merging companies need to prepare a further detailed report setting out the legal and economic aspects of the merger.

4.2.2 APPROVAL OF A MERGER

(i) *Notice*: Notice should be published at least one month in advance of the date of the meeting. Special requirements are stated for this type of meeting, as discussed previously under 3.6. Together with the notice for the shareholders' meeting, the relevant documentation as specified in art 238 of the SA Law must be made available to the shareholders and to workers' representatives among others. This documentation must include, for example, the following:

(a) the merger report;

(b) the experts' report(s) on the merger report;

(c) the report of the directors on the merger report;

(d) the annual accounts of the last three preceding years together with the relevant auditors' reports;

(e) the draft deed of incorporation of the new company, or the amendments to be included in the articles of association if one company is taking over the other(s);

(f) the articles of association of each of the companies to be merged;

(g) particulars of all the company directors, including dates of appointment as directors. Similarly, particulars of those proposed as directors as the result of the merger also need to be stated.

(ii) *Resolutions*: In the event that the resolution approving the merger is passed, additional formalities must be observed. For example, art 242 of the Law on SAs states that such a resolution must be published three times in the Commercial Registry Gazette (*Boletin Oficial del Registro Mercantil*) and also in two major newspapers where the merging companies have their registered offices. In this published notice, it must be stated that shareholders and creditors have the right to obtain copies of the full text of the resolution and the financial report relating to the merger. The merger may not take place until one month after last publication of the notice, and creditors may object, within this period until settlement of their claims is duly guaranteed.

Approval of a merger must be recorded in a deed executed before a notary public and must include the financial reports. If a new company is created as the result of the merger, the deed must include all the necessary clauses required for the incorporation of new companies (see 3.3.2). If one or more companies are taken over, the deed must contain all the amendments agreed in respect of the articles of association and details of the number and classes of shares which are to be delivered to each of the new shareholders.

The deed of merger must be duly registered in the Commercial Registry (*Registro Mercantil*). It will also be necessary to register the new company resulting from the merger, if this is the case, or to cancel the registration of those taken over. The deed is then published in the Official Gazette of the Commercial Registry. After a merger has been registered with the Commercial Registry, it is still possible to challenge its validity on the grounds that the resolution passed at the general meeting was null and voidable.

4.3   HIVE OFF OF A COMPANY ('ESCISION')

The SA Law includes, under this heading, the following transactions:

(a)   those transactions which are the converse of mergers, being the division of a dissolving company's business between two or more companies; and

(b)   those transactions which involve part or parts of the assets of a company being transferred without its being dissolved.

The asset transfers may be made either to a new or to an existing company.

In general, the provisions applicable are those stated for mergers. There are however, some specific provisions applicable only to a division of a company, (arts 252 to 259 of the Law on *Sociedades Anonimas*), for example:

(1)   The initial report on the division of the company must include additional information, *inter alia*, the amount of assets and liabilities to be transferred.

(2)   The shares of a company must be fully paid up before the division of the company takes place.

(3)   In the case of non-cash assets, a report should be obtained from one or more experts appointed by the Commercial

Registrar. The directors of the participating companies have to certify that the reports relating to non-cash assets have been produced.

4.4 SPANISH COMPETITION LAW

Competition Protection Law of 1989 (*Defensa de la Competencia*) establishes that the Ministry of Economic Affairs may, in respect to a transaction resulting in the control of a company or companies and which is likely to affect the Spanish market, refer the matter to the Court for Protection of Competition (*Tribunal de Defensa de la Competencia*) for its consideration. Article 15 of this law requires the parties involved to notify the Bureau for the Protection of Competition before the merger or acquisition occurs. The authority's silence during the period of one month will be interpreted as a tacit consent. Otherwise, the Court will submit a report to the Ministry, which must give its decision within a period of three months.

4.5 ACQUISITIONS

4.5.1 TRANSFER OF ASSETS AND LIABILITIES

Article 266 of the Law on SAs establishes that after the dissolution of a company, the liquidation period will follow, except in the case of mergers, divisions 'or any others relating to the transfer of assets and liabilities'. The last type of transaction included in this provision is one of the vehicles for purchasing a company. The purchaser may have the option to buy only some of the assets, or as in this case, may acquire all the assets and liabilities and decide to continue with the same business or change the objects and the activities of the company, or even dissolve it.

4.5.2 PURCHASE OF SHARES

The purchase of a sufficient number of shares gives the purchaser control of the company. As above, the purchaser may decide not to acquire all the shares but only a sufficient number to take control of the company. In both cases all assets and liabilities remain with the company.

The transfer of bearer shares is subject to the regulations of the Code of Commerce and they can be transferred by simple delivery of the document. The transfer of nominal shares is done by the required endorsement, at present regulated by the Exchange and Cheque Law (*Ley Cambiaria y del Cheque*). Presentation of the relevant share certificates is also required. The directors of the company are responsible for recording share transfers in the Register Book (see 3.4.3).

4.5.3 TAKEOVERS

Takeovers are usually referred to in Spain as OPA (*Oferta Publica de Adquisicion*). The framework for these operations may be found in Law 24/1988. This type of transaction provides the opportunity to purchase shares of a company which are quoted on the stock market (*Bolsa de Valores*). The acquiring company must state the minimum and maximum amount of shares which it intends to acquire and notify the National Stock Exchange Commission (*Commission Nacional del Mercado de Valores*) accordingly. It is for the National Stock Exchange Commission to confirm that the acquiring company may proceed.

Formalities applicable to takeovers: Law 24/1988, the Securities Market Act, which provides the legal framework for takeovers, has been further implemented by Royal Decree 1197/91 which lays down the formalities in respect of takeovers. In a case where the purpose is to acquire a significant percentage of control, the takeover bid must be made for a minimum amount of shares. The Decree treats a proposed acquisition of 25 per cent or more of the shares as significant. Minimum takeover bids must be made according to the percentage which is intended to be acquired. Thus, if the aim is the acquisition of 25 per cent or more of the shares the takeover bid must be for at least 10 per cent of the share capital. In the event that the aim is to acquire 50 per cent or more, the takeover bid must be for at least 75 per cent of the share capital. The procedure for the purchase of shares through a takeover bid is as follows:

(1) A bid is filed with the Commission for authorisation to proceed. If the Commission agrees, the takeover bid may be submitted to the shareholders. If the Commission denies authorisation, this decision may be appealed by initiating legal proceedings.

(2) If the Commission has authorised the bid, the shareholders of the company may proceed to consider it. They have a period of between one and two months before taking a decision. At this stage, a brochure must be published containing details of the bidder and any observations that the Commission may have issued in this respect. Within 15 days of the publication of the bid, other parties may submit competing bids. These new bids must contain an offer at least 5 per cent higher than the prior bid. The initial bidder is offered the possibility of withdrawing his bid. This is an exception to the general rule that takeover bids are generally irrevocable.

(3) After consideration by the shareholders of the company, the board of directors of the company must issue a report stating their opinion on the takeover bid. If the takeover is accepted the results must be duly published and the parties must comply with the obligations agreed in the bid.

Since the creation of the National Stock Exchange Commission (see 10.6) which exercises powers of supervision and control of the Securities Market, takeover bids have started to play a significant role in the Stock Market.

5
AGENCY, FRANCHISING AND DISTRIBUTION

5.1 INTRODUCTION

Under Spanish law, legislation provides one of the most important sources for commercial acts. The provisions of the Civil Code, Commercial Code and some specific statutes regulate much of contract law. Legal doctrine makes several classifications in respect of those regulated contracts. Economic development has brought new contracts which are only partly regulated, or not at all, although their existence has been recognised by doctrine and case law. This is the case, for example, with franchising, factoring and other contracts.

5.1.1 FREEDOM OF CONTRACT

The essential elements concerning obligations arising under a contract may be found in Book IV Civil Code (arts 1088—1314). In the case of commercial contracts, as noted above, further specific rules may be found in the Commercial Code and commercial customs. Where there are no specific rules regulating a contract, the courts have dealt with them by referring to the freedom of the parties to enter into agreements defining the terms and conditions as they deem fit, with the only restrictions the law, moral principles and public order (art 1255, Civil Code). There are several other provisions in the Civil Code reflecting this principle, which is also contained in the Code of Commerce. Article 50 states that commercial contracts shall be governed by the general rules of the common law in respect of anything which is not expressly enacted by the Code or by special commercial laws in everything relating to their formation, amendment, defences, interpretation, termination and the legal capacity of the contracting parties.

5.1.2 FORMALITIES

The general rule of Spanish law is contained in art 1278 of the Civil Code, which states that agreements shall be binding irrespective of the form in which they have been executed provided that they comply with the essential requirements for their validity, as stated by art 1261 of the Civil Code. Along the same lines, art 51(1) of the Commercial Code provides that commercial contracts shall be valid and give rise to legal obligations and rights of action, whatever the form or language in which they are made, the type of contract and the consideration.

There are exceptions to these rules, with many agreements requiring some specific form or formality necessary for their validity, for example, in the case of the incorporation of limited companies discussed in Chapter 3. But the general principle of freedom of form has been interpreted by the courts as giving further support to the view that agreements need not necessarily fall within one of those specifically defined by the existing legislation.

5.1.3 INTERPRETATION OF AGREEMENTS

Articles 1281—1289 of the Civil Code provide the general rules for the interpretation of contracts. These rules consider *inter alia* the intention of the parties before and after the execution of the agreement. The Commercial Code also contains some important provisions in this respect, for example art 57 states that commercial contracts shall be carried out and performed in good faith and that the wording of the agreement should be interpreted in accordance with its usual meaning. In interpreting those contracts not regulated or only partly regulated, the courts have given special consideration to the intention of the parties to create legal relations and have decided that in accordance with art 1258 of the Civil Code, agreements are binding not only as regards what has been expressly agreed but also in respect of those results that in their nature will follow in accordance with good faith, custom and the law.

5.2 AGENCY

5.2.1 TYPES OF AGENTS

The activities of agents have until recently been regulated

mainly by the Commercial Code. The commission agents (*Comisionista*) activities were initially taken into account in the Code of 1885. The activity of these agents is essentially sporadic as they are engaged to carry out a specific assignment. Article 244 of the Commercial Code states that a commercial commission transaction occurs when the object of a transaction is to carry out a commercial activity and the principal (*comitente*) or the agent (*comisionista*) are merchants or agents. The agent is free to agree or refuse to carry out an assignment, but needs to inform the principal if he refuses (art 248 Commercial Code). If he accepts, and then fails to carry out the obligations he undertook he will be liable for damage caused to the principal. The principal is responsible for the obligations undertaken by the agent on his behalf. In this respect, it is necessary to distinguish between situations where the agent strictly carried out his instructions, and those where he deviated from them. In the latter case, the principal is still liable but has the right to act against the agent.

In addition to the obligation of strictly carrying out the instructions received, the agent must report to the principal. This has been interpreted by case law and doctrine to include not only financial matters, but also accounting for any stock of goods and commercial documentation. In turn, the principal must pay the agent the agreed commission, plus his disbursements and lawful interest on them from the date that they were incurred by the agent.

The activities of those agents who carry out long term assignments are usually regulated by an agency contract and fall therefore into a separate category, that of the commercial agents (*Agentes*).

5.2.2 LAW 12/1992

As stated above the agency contract has been developing in practice, having as basic rules those of the Commercial Code. However, EC rules have influenced further developments. Regulation (86/633/EEC) aims to harmonise the rules of the member states which apply to self-employed agents by stating certain basic requirements, such as that the agreement must be in writing. The directive must be implemented at the latest by 1 January 1994. Spain has reacted to this directive by passing a new law, Law 12/1992 of 2 May 1992, where its provisions were included and developed further. The rules of this law will be effective from 1 January 1994 in respect of those agreements entered into before the law came into force.

The definition of agency contained in the law emphasises the independent character of the agent, who may promote and/or conclude commercial transactions on behalf of one or more principals. The activities of an agent is therefore defined in wider terms than those of the Directive, which refers to them only as 'buying and selling goods'. The Law also states that the duration of the contract may be for a definite or indefinite period of time and that the services of the agents must be remunerated. An agent (*agente*) may be an individual or corporation. The principles of this new law will be applicable to different commercial agents, but this general rule has exceptions, since some agents eg stock exchange brokers are explicitly excluded.

5.2.3   OBLIGATIONS OF THE PARTIES

The parties entering into an agency agreement may include, *inter alia*, clauses dealing with the method of accounting, duration of the contract, and the parties' obligations, which should be clearly defined. Clauses stating the agent's obligations must take into account art 9 of Law 12/1992. The law imposes a general duty on the agent to act loyally and in good faith, taking care of the interest of his principal or principals. The agent's obligations include, for example, the duty to

(a)   promote and carry out the transactions requested;
(b)   provide the principal with all the information available which may be necessary for the promotions of the transactions requested, and also in respect of third parties' insolvency;
(c)   keep independent accounts in respect of each principal.

The principal's obligation include, for example, the duty to

(a)   provide the agent in due course with the necessary quantity of brochures, price lists and other documentation required for carrying on his activities;
(b)   effect payment as agreed.

It is important to mention that the new law states that in the event of dispute the agent's address determines the court's territorial jurisdiction.

5.3 FRANCHISING

5.3.1 RULES APPLICABLE

Franchising agreements (*Contratos de Franquicia*) have deve-loped in practice out of the provisions of the Commercial Code (see 5.1). Case law has dealt on occasion with this type of contract. In judgment given by the Supreme Court on 15 May 1985 dealing with the use of a trade mark where the franchisor had allowed the franchisee to use its trade mark, the court recognised the existence of this type of contract. Legal doctrine has dealt more frequently with franchising and authorities have distinguished among several types of agreements, such as:

(a) 'shop within a shop' franchising where some specific and particular goods are sold within a department store;

(b) franchising of production where the essential element is the quality and reputation of the goods.

In addition it should be noted that EC rules are applicable to,eg Regs No 4087/88 relating to the application of art 85.3 EEC in relation to franchising agreements.

5.3.2 STANDARD CLAUSES

Taking into account the applicable rules which have been briefly mentioned above, franchising agreements may be defined as those entered between a franchisor (*franquiciador*) and a franchisee (*franquiciado*) by which the former allows the latter to use trade marks or another specific distinctive name or method to sell a particular product or service in return for a payment.

The following are among clauses normally included:

(a) clear particulars of the parties entering into the agreement;

(b) assignment of a territory granted to the franchisee;

(c) duration of the contract and procedure for dealing with remaining stock at the end of the contract;

(d) obligations of the parties including terms of payment and cost liabilities (ie disbursements), and penalties in the event of default;

(e) trade name and trade marks designs: the franchisor will normally guarantee the validity of his rights over his mark or distinctive name and therefore the fact that the franchisee will be able to carry out his activities without any challenge in this respect;

(f)   non-competition clauses;

(g)   price of the merchandise;

(h)   jurisdiction.

Naturally clauses dealing with the obligations of the parties need particular attention. The franchisor will normally deal with publicity and promotion of the product. He will also provide the franchisee with all the background, manuals training and generally all the necessary information to carry out the business, and the franchisee will be required to keep this information confidential. The franchisee will usually be requested to maintain the franchisor's standards and public image.

The franchisee will normally have to make a down payment (*pago de entrada*) and also comply with any other payment provisions as agreed, eg a payment on the profits obtained. The franchisee must also comply with the obligations undertaken in respect of regular information to be provided to the franchisor. The latter normally reserves his rights of inspection. In the event of breach of the agreement, the contract will be terminated and compensation may be claimed through the ordinary courts, for example, if the contract stated that the franchisee would sell exclusively products of the franchisor but he then sold other products as well.

5.4   DISTRIBUTION

5.4.1   INTRODUCTION

Spanish law does specifically regulate this type of agreement. The general rules applicable to commercial contracts and those of the Civil Code relating to the formation of contracts provide the legal framework. These agreements provide a vehicle to resell goods in Spain and form part of commercial practice. The courts have dealt with them from time to time and their opinion may provide another source to be considered for some cases, such as exclusive distribution agreements (*distribucion en exclusiva*).

5.4.2 STANDARD CLAUSES

Careful drafting of a contract is required so that the obligations of the parties are clearly defined. In this respect it is important to clarify that the distributor is acting independently and assumes the risks of transactions which he carries out.

Distribution contracts will include clauses covering the following matters:

(a) the parties to the agreement: the party appointing the distributor (*cedente*) and the distributor (*distribuidor*);

(b) assignment of territory;

(c) price of the merchandise including notice for increasing prices;

(d) details of the use of any patents and trade marks: the distributor normally acknowledges and confirms that the patent rights and trade mark rights are under licence. The distributor needs to advise the other party immediately of any patent or trade mark infringement and further, initiate proceedings and take necessary action to stop any infringement (see 1.1.2);

(e) duties of the parties, including the restrictions agreed on the distributor, for example whether or not he is authorised to appoint sub-distributors;

(f) duration of the contract and notices required for termination of the agreement;

(g) consequences as to termination, for example, outstanding unpaid invoices shall become payable immediately (or within a period of time as agreed by the parties).

(h) minimum sales;

(i) transfer of title of the merchandise, including details of documentation to be submitted;

(j) terms relating to the delivery of the merchandise, including details as to which party will be liable for arranging transport, packaging and insurance;

(k) confidentiality: the distributor will normally be required not to divulge at any time any confidential information in relation to the company's affairs or business or method of carrying on business;

(l) *force majeure*;

(m)   termination;
(n)   jurisdiction.

The obligations of the distributor may include the following:

(a)   to attend fairs to promote the products;
(b)   to keep the other party informed of the sales, market conditions, clients' details etc;
(c)   to give the other party access to the accounts and stock records;
(d)   to maintain an inventory of sales including sales aids i.e. brochures and similar literature.

The obligations of the party appointing the distributor may include for example the following:

(a)   to use all reasonable endeavours to assist in the promotion of sales of the product;
(b)   in the event of faulty products, to remedy the defects or supply a substitute in exchange for the returned product, or to issue a credit note;
(c)   to comply with the delivery periods agreed.

6
PROPERTY AND SUCCESSION

6.1 INTRODUCTION

Article 333 of the Civil Code classifies all things which are capable of being appropriated as either movables or immovables, a distinction important in Spanish law, which is based on the civil law system. This distinction is particularly important in connection with the transfer of immovable property and the formalities for doing so. However, the transfer of some movable property may also require specific formalities, as in the case of trade marks. Furthermore, the economic importance of some movable and immovable property resulted in special regulation, as with the law on cheques and documentary credit documentation in the case of movable property, or the laws regulating rural property in the case of immovable property.

Article 348 of the Civil Code defines the rights of an owner in respect of property as the right to use it and to transfer it.

6.2 MOVABLES AND IMMOVABLES

6.2.1 MOVABLES

Article 335 of the Civil Code states that property not included in art 334 (see 6.2.2) must be considered movable. It also includes in this category all things which may be moved from one place to another without detriment to the place to which they were affixed. Article 464 of the Civil Code contains the general rules as to the title of movable property and states that possession will be deemed as title for movable property.

6.2.2 IMMOVABLES

Article 334 of the Civil Code lists the property which is classified as immovable property. It includes:

(a) land and buildings;
(b) trees, plants (and fruits) planted in the soil and forming

part of a real estate;
(c)   everything that is affixed permanently and cannot be detached without detriment to its surroundings or to itself;
(d)   mines;
(e)   water front construction.

6.3   PURCHASE OF PROPERTY

Rights over land and buildings are classified as immovable property. Their transfer requires compliance with prescribed legal formalities.

6.3.1   PRELIMINARY STEPS

Before signing any agreement it is important to deal with some preliminary verifications. These will protect the prospective buyer against some serious problems and loss. As a basic guideline the following points must be considered:

(1)   Investigation of the title of the property: it is not unusual to find that there have been several previous 'owners' of a property who have not dealt with registration at the Land Registry. If they are not the registered owners they cannot transfer good title to the property which is being sold.

(2)   Verification in the Land Registry of the property details, as far as possible.

(3)   Verification at the Land Registry that the property is free of all charges and encumbrances such as mortgages: this may protect the buyer against a mortgage created by, for example, the developer. (see 6.3.3 and 9.2.2).

(4)   It is also important to check that local authority regulations and general planning law have been complied with so far as the construction of the property is concerned (see 11.2).

(5)   It is also advisable to verify that there is no tenant in the property and that vacant possession will be available upon completion of the contract.

(6)   In the case of flats, and some villas which share some common parts, it is important to check if the purchaser is assuming other liabilities such as maintenance charges etc.

The above are very general guidelines and any prospective buyer should take into account the characteristics of the specific property concerned.

6.3.2 DRAFTING CONSIDERATIONS

The transfer of immovable property must be executed through a public deed (*Escritura Publica*) followed by payment of taxes and registration of the deed in the appropriate Land Registry. For a variety of reasons the parties sometimes execute private agreements; these are valid as between the parties but are not sufficient for the purposes of transferring the property.

Any sale/purchase agreement must accurately describe the property being sold and clearly identify the seller and the buyer. The agreement must also state that the property is sold free of all charges and encumbrances, and should specify the parties' respective liabilities as to taxes and any outstanding payments. Of course the drafting of an agreement will take into account the specific circumstances of the transaction but commonly includes a provision to the effect that if there is no completion due to the vendor's default, he should return the deposit plus legal interest, whereas if it is due to the purchaser's default the vendor will keep the deposit.

To illustrate the above, a Private Agreement may be in the following form:

Place and date of the agreement
Identification of the parties

Whereas:
I [X] is the owner of the following property: (full description of the property, including boundaries) Title: full details, including Land Registry details.

II [O] is interested in acquiring the property described above.

IT IS HEREBY AGREED:
First: [X] sells the property _____ to [O]

Second: The price agreed is _____ which will be paid as follows:

Third: The sale/purchase deed will be executed before the Public Notary when the purchaser pays the total amount of the price agreed.

Fourth: All the expenses and taxes relating to this agreement will be paid by _____.

Fifth: Should the purchaser not comply with his obligations of effecting payment within the period agreed in the second clause, [X] will be able to demand immediate payment, or, to terminate the contract without the obligation of returning the monies paid, these being retained as compensation for damages.

Sixth: The property is sold free of any lease or occupants, and there are no outstanding payments in connection with rates, taxes, including local taxes;

Seventh: Both parties undertake expressly to submit any matters in connection with this agreement to the Courts of _____.

IN WITNESS of which the parties have duly executed this agreement which is delivered on the date and place before written.

6.3.3   DEED FORMALITIES AND REGISTRATION

As stated above the sale/purchase deed needs to be executed before a Spanish public notary, who will ensure that it complies with the required formalities. From 6 August 1993, notaries will also need to obtain information from the Land Registry in respect of real property which is to be transferred or where a charge is to be created against the property, unless the buyer declares that he does not require this information (see 9.2.1). However, the notary will not guarantee the accuracy of the statements made by the parties and will only certify that the parties have signed the agreement properly. This should be borne in mind, so that completion should not take place until both parties are satisfied with the terms of the agreement and, in particular, the buyer has made all the necessary preliminary enquiries.

If one of the parties will not be present at this stage, it may be possible to transfer the title by granting a power of attorney to someone, usually a lawyer, who will represent the absent party.

Before proceeding to registration there are a number of taxes to be paid on the purchase/sale of a property. These taxes are as follows:

(a)   VAT or transfer tax;

(b)   a local tax (*Arbitrio Municipal de Plusvalia*). This is usually referred to as *Plusvalia*, but should not be confused with Capital Gains Tax (see 8.2.2).

The vendor becomes liable to a tax of 35 per cent on the capital gains produced on the sale of the property. As the result of some recent amendments to the law, 10 per cent of the price paid may be retained by the purchaser and lodged with the Spanish Revenue on account of the capital gains payable by the vendor.

The above provisions do not apply where:

(a)   the owner is an individual;

(b)   the property was acquired more than 21 years prior to the sale; and

(c)   no improvements have been carried out during that time.

After the sale/purchase has been signed before the public notary, the deed should be registered with the Land Registry (*Registro de la Propiedad*). This is an essential step and cannot be omitted, in spite of the provisions of Royal Decree 1558/92 (see 9.2.1).

Those owners who are non-resident should bear in mind that they need to appoint a fiscal representative in Spain to represent them in dealing with the Spanish authorities in respect of their tax liabilities.

6.4   FREEHOLD PROPERTY OF APARTMENTS

As stated above, in the case of flats, despite the fact that the property is freehold there will be some restrictions relating to the common parts of the building. The important principles as stated by the law (*Ley de Propiedad Horizontal*), deal with the security and maintenance of the building, insurance, representation and mutual respect among owners etc. In addition, the co-owners enter into agreements in respect of the common parts of the building (*Estatutos*), in relation to the use of the building, services, expenses, organisation and representation of the co-owners, repairs etc. The common parts of a building are those which are classified as such for example, stairs, lifts, and corridors. Sometimes tax legislation has treated some parts of a building as common by reason of their purpose, for example in the case of a conference room or reception room.

In general terms the law states that each owner has exclusive property in respect of his apartment but also has a part share as stated in the sale/purchase deed, relating to the common parts of the building. This part is relevant in order to specify the owner's contribution to the general maintenance expenses and also in order to specify the owner's rights respecting these common parts, which may have to be considered in the case of expropriation or in respect of voting at general meetings.

6.5 RENTING PROPERTY

When property is rented the parties agree the relevant terms in a rental contract. In order to be protected in the event of a dispute it is essential to set out clearly the terms agreed to such as the duration of the agreement.

The tenant's rights will normally be stated in a tenancy agreement. A tenancy agreement should specify clearly the following:

(a) parties to the agreement;

(b) the rent payable;

(c) expenses and in general all the liabilities of the parties in particular those relating to:

 (i) maintenance of the property;

 (ii) payment of the local rates;

 (iii) payment of electricity, water and telephone bills;

(d) (usually) a specified duration date; and

(e) a deposit as a guarantee in respect of the property and furniture, in the case of furnished accommodation. The amount of money required as a deposit will vary but it will normally be at least equivalent to one month's rent.

In any event even if the agreement has a specified duration the owner of the property will still need a court order to evict the tenant in the event of breach of contract or if the tenant refuses to leave. Note that protection granted to tenants differs for those whose tenancies were entered into before May 1985. In accordance with earlier law the tenant may be entitled to transfer his right to his children living with him. These tenants are also protected against increases of rent.

In respect of commercial leases (*Arrendamiento de Locales de Negocio*), the tenant may have the right to assign his rights (*traspaso*), provided that the owner of the property agrees. Before paying any deposit it is important for an assignee to verify some preliminary details, as to whether there is a valid licence to carry on the activities of the business, and if new activities are going to be carried out whether these may be included in the existing licence or not. In the event that a new licence is required it is always better to check with the local authority as to the requirements and time involved. In practice, this may be a lengthy process to overcome before any business activity may be carried out, which is certainly an important element to consider.

It should also be mentioned that there may be a lease not only of the premises but also of the business (*Arrendamiento de Industria o Negocio*). Case law has interpreted this as being the case where the business activities may be carried on immediately by the tenant because the lease includes the premises and all the necessary machinery, furniture etc.

6.6 SUCCESSION

6.6.1 INTRODUCTION

The death of a person results in a complex transfer of assets and debts. Article 659 of the Civil Code states that the estate at the death of a deceased includes all assets, rights and obligations continuing after the death. Inheritance is regulated by law, and there are restrictions as to the provisions which can be included in a will, for example, there are certain heirs by law (*Herederos Forzosos*) who are protected from exclusion.

The practitioner may have to deal with both testamentary and intestate succession, under art 658 of the Civil Code, which also states that an estate can devolve partly in accordance with the wishes of the deceased and partly in accordance with the applicable legal provisions.

6.6.2 TYPES OF SUCCESSION

Wills: Article 667 of the Civil Code defines a will as an act through which a person disposes of part or all of his assets after death (*Testamento*). A will under Spanish law is essentially a personal act and the testator may revoke it at any time. If the deceased has not made any testamentary arrangement or if these arrangements only deal with part of his assets or the will is not valid, the estate devolves inheritance in accordance with the Spanish laws of succession.

In respect of heirs by law, the Civil Code provides that only one-third of the estate can be freely disposed of. The estate is divided into three equal parts:

(1) One third must be left to heirs by law (children) in equal shares.

(2) As to a further third, the testator may choose to benefit one (or more) of these heirs by law as he wishes.

(3) The final third can be freely disposed of to anyone the deceased chooses.

For example, X, having three children may by will deal with his estate as follows:

(a) one-third of the estate to the children in three equal shares;

(b) one-third of the estate to benefit one of the three children;

(c) one-third of the estate for his spouse.

Rights of inheritance devolve on the children of an heir who has predeceased his parents. So in the above example, if at the time of X's death, only two out of his three children were alive but the third child had surviving children, these will assume the rights of their parent to inherit from their grandfather.

There are different types of will which may be valid in Spanish inheritance law. The most usual one, *testamento abierto*, is executed before a public notary and signed in his presence; it is then registered in a central registry in Madrid called the *Registro Central de Ultima Voluntad.*

Foreigners with assets in Spain should be advised to make a separate Spanish will dealing with any Spanish assets so that their heirs can receive this inheritance independently of any other assets situated elsewhere. This will enable the heirs to apply for the grant of probate in Spain in respect of the Spanish assets, without being affected by delays occurring in respect of any other application for a grant of probate in another country.

Intestate Succession: Spanish law provides specific and detailed rules relating to the devolution of the estate. The order of succession depends on their relationship to the deceased, with closest relatives excluding the more remote. Article 915 *et seq* of the Civil Code contains the rules as to the order of succession. The children are the first heirs (art 931), followed by the ascendants (parents, grandparents etc), all without prejudice to the life interest in one-third of the estate given by law to the surviving spouse. If the deceased has no surviving ascendants, the surviving spouse, or if none, other relatives such as siblings, or their children, may be the beneficiaries.

It is important to note that regional laws also establish some further specific rules in connection with inheritance (*Derecho Foral*) but given the restrictions of this work, these detailed provisions are not dealt with here.

6.6.3 INHERITANCE CLAIMS

Acceptance of Inheritance

In accordance with Article 1006 of the Civil Code, beneficiaries become heirs as soon as they accept the inheritance. Acceptance may be conditional or unconditional. In the latter case, heirs will have to meet the liabilities arising from the estate not only out of the assets inherited but also with their own.

Acceptance of an inheritance must comply with the formalities established by law (art 1011 of the Civil Code), as follows:

(a) acceptance by means of a deed executed before a public notary. This will normally take place when the deceased has executed a will;

(b) acceptance before the court, when the deceased dies intestate.

The testator may have appointed one or more people (*Albacea*) to deal with the administration of the estate and to carry out his last wishes, although this is by no means a requirement.

Foreigners without a Spanish Will

In order to make a claim in respect of Spanish assets, the heirs will have to provide evidence of their inheritance rights. As a general rule, Spanish law recognises wills which are valid under the laws of the nationality of the testator. The usual procedure will entail a deed executed before a public notary and the following documentation will be required:

(a) a copy of the death certificate;
(b) a copy of the marriage certificate (if applicable);
(c) a certified copy of the grant of probate;
(d) a copy of the will (if applicable).

All of the above documentation needs to be translated into Spanish and authenticated with the Seal of the Hague Apostille duly affixed. In the UK this can be done through the Foreign and Commonwealth Office.

Once the deed of acceptance of inheritance is executed, inheritance tax should be paid, or if not due, this fact needs to be duly certified by the tax authorities. After the tax procedure is completed the relevant registrations should take place, for example at the Land Registry.

6.6.4 INHERITANCE TAX

As stated above the authorities will not allow any changes as to the title of property if they do not have evidence that the heirs have paid their inheritance tax or provided evidence that they are exempt from such payment. Non-residents have to pay tax according to the Spanish tax rules if the property is located in Spain.

Inheritance tax is applied according to the value of the assets inherited and the relationship between the deceased and his heirs. The first two million pesetas are exempt in the case of direct heirs, such as children and spouse. There are other exemptions available, such as heirs under the age of 21 may have an exemption of up to six million pesetas. Spanish inheritance tax is then applied according to a scale which starts at 7.6 per cent on the first million pesetas, rises to 24.99 per cent on 100 million pesetas, and

34 per cent on excess of this amount. Heirs' existing assets are taken into account and those who are better off will end up paying more tax, as the pre-existing wealth of the beneficiary is a multiple applied to the tax charges based on kinship.

7
IMMIGRATION AND EMPLOYMENT

7.1 IMMIGRATION

7.1.1 NON-EC NATIONALS

Non-EC nationals need, as a general rule, to have a valid passport and a visa in order to enter Spain. However, there are certain exceptions in respect of visas which have been granted through international treaties to certain nationals. One of the most important examples is that of nationals from South American countries who do not require a visa provided that they stay for no more than 90 days. Migrants intending to take up employment will need to both have a resident's and a work permit. There are different kinds of permit, and some may be granted on temporary visas or for self-employment. Both employees and the self-employed must comply with social security rules.

There are no specific rules as to the requirement for obtaining a work permit. It is usually pointed out that the creation of some employment for Spanish people would be helpful, but this is not always an essential requirement in practice. In the case of those working for an employer, the contract of employment will have to be submitted as evidence to the Spanish authorities, and in the case of the self-employed they will normally be required to provide evidence that they have the necessary means to invest in the business.

A work permit can be renewed after each expiration, even if the employee has been absent from Spain from time to time.

Application should be made at the Spanish Embassy or consulate in the applicant's home country before arriving in Spain.

7.1.2   EC NATIONALS

From 1 January 1993, the rules regarding the free movement of labour in EC member states came into force in Spain, with the result that nationals of EC countries do not require work permits to work in Spain. However, EC nationals are still required to apply for a resident's permit (*Tarjeta de Residencia Comunitaria*). The following documentation will normally be required:

(a)   a copy of the employment contract;
(b)   a passport;
(c)   a medical certificate;
(d)   three photographs.

The permit granted will normally be valid for five years, unless the employment contract is for less than one year. In any event this permit is renewable.

EC Nationals can also acquire self-employment permits and the following will normally be required:

(a)   a passport;
(b)   a certificate of good conduct;
(c)   a medical certificate;
(d)   three photographs; and
(e)   a report on the proposed investment.

7.1.3   BUSINESS OR PROFESSIONAL LICENCES

In all cases both non-EC nationals and EC nationals who wish to run their own business will need to have a professional or business licence. In the case of those who intend to open a shop or a restaurant, it is important to remember that local authorities will require compliance with particular regulations, and a special licence to open will need to be obtained (*Licencia de Apertuna*). In order to grant these authorisations the local authorities will check compliance with any special rules which are applicable, such as health regulations if there are noxious fumes or noise. In addition, all the necessary registrations with the tax authorities, social security and VAT must be complied with.

7.2   EMPLOYMENT LAW

7.2.1   INTRODUCTION

The main sources of Spanish employment law are the

Constitutional rules, and some other laws of which the most important is the Employees' Statute (*Estatuto de los Trabajadores*) of 1980. In addition, the regional governments have been given special powers to deal with employment matters.

Employment placement is dealt with by the National Employment Institute (*Instituto Nacional de Empleo*), a department of the Ministry of Labour and Social Security. These authorities are in charge of maintaining a register of those available for employment and employers are required to check with them when considering employing someone who is not senior or technical staff. However, employers are not necessarily required to hire the registered unemployed person.

7.2.2 EMPLOYMENT AGREEMENTS

In every employment agreement there are some basic rights even if there is no written agreement. In determining whether there is an employment relationship or not, the courts have conclusively decided that this is the case when a person works for somebody else and receives payment for his services while having a subordinate and not an independent role. The fact that there may sometimes be some flexibility does not necessarily mean that a worker is self-employed: if there is, for example, lack of independence.

If in a particular case it is concluded that there is or was in fact an employment agreement between the parties, as opposed to a commercial relationship, legal consequences will follow, for example, that the employer will be liable for compensation for unfair dismissal, and that the courts having jurisdiction in the event of a dispute will be the labour courts. It is therefore advisable to define the position of the parties clearly. In the case of an agency contract it will be important to clarify that there is a commercial relationship by stating the independence of the agent, who will have his own business licence, his own invoices with VAT and who will assume the risks of the transactions, in that he may suffer deductions from his commission of any unpaid amounts of money (see 5.2.1).

7.2.3 EMPLOYEE'S RIGHTS

The basic rights of employees are mainly contained in the Spainish Constitution and the Employees' Statute (*Estatuto de los*

Trabajadores). Article 4 of the *Estatuto de los Trabajadores* lists the basic rights of the workers, which are reflected in different articles of the Spanish Constitution. These rights are as follows:

(1) The right to work and to have free choice of profession or trade: this right is reflected in art 35 of the Constitution which states that all Spaniards have the duty to work and the right of employment, and also to free choice of profession or trade, to advancement through their work and through sufficient remuneration for the satisfaction of their needs and those of their families.

(2) The right to freely join a trade union: this right is reflected in art 28 of the Constitution, which also states that the law may limit the exercise of this right or make exceptions to it in the case of the armed forces or other bodies subject to military discipline and shall regulate its exercise by Civil Servants. Trade union freedom includes the right to found a union and to join the union of one's choice as well as the right of trade unions to form confederations, to found international trade union organisations or to become members thereof. Nobody may be compelled to join a trade union.

(3) The right to collective negotiations (*negociacion colectiva*): this right is reflected in art 37 of the Constitution which guarantees the right to collective negotiations between workers and employers' representatives as well as the binding force of the agreements.

(4) The right to strike: this right is recognised in art 28.2 of the Constitution, which also states that the law regulating the exercise of this right shall establish the guarantees necessary to ensure the maintenance of essential community services.

(5) The right of meeting: art 21 of the Constitution establishes the right to peaceful assembly without arms. It also states that the exercise of this right shall not require prior authorisation but that in the case of meetings in public places and of demonstrations, prior notification shall be given to the authorities, who may ban them only when there are well founded grounds for expecting a breach of public order involving danger to persons or property.

(6) The right to participate within a company: this is also reflected in the Constitution in art 1.9.2, where it is stated that the public authorities shall promote the various forms

of participation within companies and shall encourage co-operative societies by means of appropriate legislation.

(7) Further, employees have the right as well as the duty to work for their employer. They also have a right to training and promotion, and they may not be in any way discriminated against on account of sex, marital status, age, race, social condition, religious or political beliefs, membership of a trade union, etc. This right is established in art 14 of the Spanish Constitution.

(8) There is a right to physical and moral integrity.

(9) An employee has the right to privacy and due consideration for his dignity.

(10) Employees have the right to receive the salary agreed or established by law.

(11) The right to enforce claims in connection with the employment agremeent: this right is reflected in art 24 of the Constitution, which establishes the right of free access to the courts to enforce rights.

In addition to the above, employees have additional rights contained specifically in their employment agreements.

On the other hand, these rights are counterbalanced by employees' basic obligations which include the duty:

(a) to fulfil their obligations in good faith and with diligence;

(b) to comply with security and health measures;

(c) to comply with orders and instructions given by their employers;

(d) to improve productivity, and

(e) to carry out the specific obligations as stated in their employment agreements.

Employee Representation: Employees' interests are represented within each place of work through special bodies: workers' councils (*Comites de Empresa*) (when more than 50 employees) or employee delegates (*delegados de empresa*) if fewer than 50. In the former case there will be at least five members, in the latter case there may be only one delegate if the workplace has less than 30 employees. The employee representatives have the right to receive information and issue reports, and they play a very important role for purposes of taking certain decisions such as personnel restructuring, mergers and takeovers etc. These representatives are chosen by the employees at a workplace directly. In addition, employee interests are represented through union representatives who will liaise in a company both with employees and management. These representatives are chosen by the unions, but union delegates are elected by employees affiliated to the union in a workplace.

Basic Employee Protection: Employees' rights include the right to minimum wages and place a limit on working hours. The Employees' Statute provides the basic rules which are complemented by numerous other rules. The general rules provide:

(1)   There is a maximum of 40 working hours per week and each hour worked over the 40 hours is considered overtime.

(2)   Overtime is voluntary, unless otherwise agreed individually or collectively.

(3)   When employment is for less that 40 hours a week payment shall be proportional.

(4)   The minimum annual holiday is 30 calendar days.

Salaries are divided in three parts which will include a basic salary, a supplemental (for example production incentives) and extraordinary payments (extra monthly payments to be made at Christmas and in the summer). There is minimum wage fixed annually after consulation with the major trade unions and management. At the present time the minimum wage fixed by the government is 58,530 pesetas. However, there are several other minimum wages which are higher that have been agreed separately by collective bargaining by different sectors of workers at national level.

7.3   TERMINATION OF EMPLOYMENT AGREEMENTS

7.3.1   RECENT DEVELOPMENTS

The general rule of having employment agreements which are for an indefinite term has had as one of its consequences the fact that redundancies are very costly for employers, due to the fact that employment can be terminated only on the grounds specified by the *Estatuto de los Trabajadores*. As a result new legislation has been passed creating the possibility of entering into temporary employment contracts, and also providing some incentives to employers to create jobs. Temporary employment agreements are those agreements with a duration of three years or less. These contracts are usually authorised in circumstances where there are some specific services to be performed. The aim is to help small businesses and combat unemployment.

Some recent laws relating to incentives for employers are as follows:

- The Decree awarding grants to employers offering permanent jobs (6 August 1992). These regulations implement Law 22/1992 on Urgent Measures for the Creation of Employment
- The Decree relating to Corporation Tax Allowances for the Creation of Jobs (14 October 1992). These rules relate to the creation of jobs for disabled workers and are intended to implement Law 22/1992 or Urgent Measures for the Creation of Employment.

7.3.2 TERMINATION UNDER THE EMPLOYEES' STATUTE

Termination of employment is governed by the Employees' Statute (*Estatuto de los Trabajadores*), which sets out several grounds *inter alia* the following:

(a) Agreement of the parties: this includes any of the causes stated in the agreement unless these clauses reflect the employer's abuse of his position;

(b) termination of the work or service which was the object of the agreement;

(c) death, serious injury or serious incapacity of the employee;

(d) retirement of the employee;

(e) death, retirement or disability of the employer;

(f) *force majeure* resulting in permanent impossibility for carrying out the work;

(g) technological or economic causes which result in the permanent closure of the industry, commerce or service;

(h) dismissal by the employer;

(i) unilateral decision of the employee based on the employer's breach of the agreement (see below).

7.3.3   INTERPRETATION OF GROUNDS FOR TERMINATION

The *Estatuto de Los Trabajadores* art 50 gives an employee the right to terminate his employment where the employer introduces substantial changes which are prejudicial to his professional development or his dignity. Another ground for termination is delay in payment of salary and any other serious breach of the employer's obligations. In any of these circumstances, the employee has the right to receive the same compensation as in the case of unfair dismissal. Case law has established that in order for this claim to succeed, it has been normally required that the employee continue working for the employer unless there are serious reasons preventing him from doing so, eg where he is at risk physically.

So far as the dismissal of the employee by the employer is concerned, the law requires a serious and wilful breach of obligations by the employee. The agreement is so breached where there are frequent and unjustified absences and lack of punctuality, or other actions by the employee such as verbal or physical attacks on the employer or wilful and continual decrease in productivity. The court normally requires wilful conduct by the employee, and that it was not the result of a third party's conduct. Absences and lack of punctuality have not been considered by the courts automatically as grounds for dismissal—it depends on the circumstances. Where there is good cause to dismiss, the employer must give the employee notice in writing, setting out the reasons for the decision and the date from which the dismissal will take place. In the event that the court decides that this decision was null, the employee will be reinstated in his work and will be entitled to the salary which should otherwise have been paid.

Labour courts have played an important role in the interpretation of the grounds for termination as identified by the Employees' Statute, particularly in dealing with the grounds for dismissal. If the employee challenges his dismissal the court will have to be satisfied that all the formalities were complied with, and will require evidence in respect of the cause relied on for dismissal. For example, in the case of disciplinary dismissal where many different grounds may be included, such as unexplained absences, the court will require evidence that notice of dismissal was duly given. If the court concludes that the dismissal was a violation of the employee's rights, it may order that the employee should be reinstated and compensation paid.

7.3.4 FORCE MAJEURE

Labour courts have also dealt with the interpretation of *force majeure* as a ground for termination of a contract. The *Estatuto de los Trabajadores* only refers to it as a possible ground for the termination or suspension of the contract but does not define the concept. The courts have generally interpreted it as meaning the same as the old law regulating employment contracts (art 76.6), which defined *force majeure* as an extraordinary, unforeseeable and inevitable event having the consequence it is impossible for work to continue within a workplace. The old employment law also included other causes such as fires, earthquakes, war, explosions, floods etc.

7.3.5 REDUNDANCY

General Terms: Redundancy terms are usually negotiated between employers and employees. This is, in fact, the only way to terminate employment if there is no clear evidence for claiming one of the causes included in the Employees' Statute for termination of agreements. Labour law provides that the maximum payment in a case of unfair dismissal is 45 days' salary for each year of service up to a maximum of 42 months. However, these terms would not normally be applied in the case of senior staff where negotiation is, as a rule, preferable to court proceedings. If a case does get to court, the court will award maximum compensation of 29 days per year worked with a maximum of 12 months.

Collective Redundancies: It is necessary to negotiate collective redundancies and/or lay-off, and employers must comply with a special procedure. This procedure includes the following:

(a) preparation of a detailed report including the technological or financial reasons why the company is considering the collective dismissal;
(b) negotiations with the employees' representatives;
(c) negotiations with the labour authorities.

Article 51 of the Employees' Statute has been generally interpreted as giving the workers' representatives (*Comite de*

Empresa) and the employers the power to reach an agreement in respect of staff reductions and other measures such as laid-off employees. In such an event the labour authorities must ratify these agreements but have no power to revise them.

7.4   SOCIAL SECURITY

Employers must pay social security contributions. Some of the most important services provided by Spanish social security are as follows:

(a)   health care;
(b)   temporary incapacity benefits (illness or accident);
(c)   disability benefits;
(d)   unemployment benefit;
(e)   retirement benefit;
(f)   death benefit and survival pensions;
(g)   family benefits.

Article 41 of the Spanish Constitution lays out the principles under which further legislation has been enacted. It provides:

'The public authorities shall maintain a public social security system for all citizens which will guarantee adequate social assistance and benefits in needy situations, especially in cases of unemployment. Supplementary assistance and benefits shall be optional.'

Social security contributions are payable with respect to all employees and that includes both native Spanish employees and foreigners working in Spain. Employers are responsible for collecting and paying employees' contributions through wage deductions. Employers must pay social security contributions and these vary in accordance with the category of employment. As a general guideline it is possible to state that the contribution to social security in respect of the general quota is a rate of 29.30 per cent. This is applied to salaries with 24.40 per cent being paid by an employer and 4.90 per cent by the employee.

As stated above, the government provides subsidies to employers in some cases, for example a subsidy is payable to those employers who have provided employment for young qualified trainees who qualified within the previous four years.

The administration of the Social Security systems is in the hands of the central and regional governments. Private agencies are also authorised to participate provided that they abide by the restrictions imposed, such as, that they remain non-profit making organisations. It must be remembered that labour laws are complex and that there are different rules according to types of employment. So far as social security provisions are concerned, there are some special rules for contributions and benefit applicable to workers in specific areas such as agriculture, the civil service, domestic employment etc.

8
TAXATION LAW

8.1 THE EC HARMONISATION PROCESS

Membership of the EC has brought some important changes in the structure of the Spanish tax system, to a large extent reflecting the aims of Spanish economic policy since its entry into the EC. Among the most important changes adopted, are:
- (a) with regard to indirect taxes, the introduction of VAT;
- (b) the decision of the Constitutional Court of 20 February 1989 which held that family members may be taxed separately;
- (c) improvement of the tax administration system with the aim of implementing the reforms and also combatting tax fraud;
- (d) liberalisation of the system regarding the international movement of capital within the EC, as discussed in Chapter 10;
- (e) new company law provisions.

No doubt the system will undergo further developments to conform to EC fiscal harmonisation. One of the most recent changes is the increase of the standard rate of VAT to 15 per cent in line with EC harmonisation measures, which was introduced on 1 August 1992. (This was the second increase in the standard rate of VAT, as on 1 January 1992 it had been raised from 12 per cent to 13 per cent.)

8.2 DIRECT TAXES

8.2.1 INCOME TAX

The basic rules with regard to personal income tax are provided by the Individual Income Tax Act (*Ley de Impuesto Sobre la Renta de las Personas Fisicas*) which came into force in January 1992, plus additional rules implementing this law.

The legal framework distinguishes between residents and non-residents.

Residents

An individual is presumed to be resident in Spain for tax purposes if he is physically present in Spain for more than 183 days or if the main place of professional or business activities or other economic interest is situated in Spain, or his spouse and minor children qualify as Spanish residents under the same conditions. The person affected by this presumption may prove the contrary to the authorities. The effect of being resident in Spain for tax purposes is that the individual is liable for personal tax in respect of his worldwide income.

The presumption introduced by Law 18/1991 is that income tax is based on an individual rather than a family tax unit. In practice, the family unit may choose whether or not to file a joint return and if the latter is the case, all income must be reported in the same return.

Taxable income will include income from the following:

(1) *Income from employment*—includes all kinds of benefit in cash or in kind such as salary, rent-free accommodation or a free supply or use of a car (benefit in kind), pensions, director remunerations, travel expenses, allowances etc.

(2) *Income from capital*—includes income from movable and immovable property which is not related to the taxpayer's business or professional activities.

(3) *Business or professional income*—includes profits obtained as a result of carrying on a trade and/or professional income. A trade may include, for example, the production or supply of goods or services and covers farming, mining, construction and services. Professional services are those provided in the course of a profession or artistic activities.

(4) *Capital gains*—includes profits arising from the transfer of property as will be discussed under 8.2.2.

(5) Income under fiscal transparency regime—as the result of the new rules, resident members of transparent companies will be taxed on the profits after deducting losses in accordance with the rules given by the formation contract. In the absence of such rules these will be distributed in equal

parts. The fiscal transparency regime applies only to certain companies such as those in which more than 50 per cent of the capital is owned by a family group and certain professional legal organisations (for example, where all the members are directly or indirectly engaged in a particular professional activity).

Exemptions

- There are certain exemptions from income tax such as, for example, lottery prizes, disability pensions for public servants, public compensations to victims of terrorism, university grants and other exemptions granted in favour of residents.
- Residents also have the benefit of family credits which are available in accordance with the family circumstances such as, for example, if the taxpayer has dependent children, dependent parents with an annual income not exceeding the annual minimum salary, etc.

The tax period is for a calendar year which ends on 31 December. Taxpayers must complete an annual income tax return and file it with the local office.

Non-residents

Those individuals who are non-resident for tax purposes are liable for income tax only in respect of Spanish income. The personal income tax rate for non-resident taxpayers is 25 per cent, except for capital gains which as will be discussed is at a rate of 35 per cent. These rates are subject to the provisions of any applicable Double Taxation Agreements.

Non-residents must appoint a local tax representative who must sign and file an annual return.

8.2.2 CAPITAL GAINS TAX (*IMPUESTO POR INCREMENTO DEL PATRIMONIO*)

There is no special capital gains tax as such in Spain. In general, liability for capital gains tax arises when there is a difference between the value at the time of acquisition and the sale price of assets. Broadly, capital gains are calculated in accordance with the same rules for residents and non-residents and the basis of the calculations is the length of time that the seller owned a property. The new tax rules have exempted from gains the sale of movable property by residents of EC countries, but there are exceptions, for example, this will not apply to income derived in some of the territories designated as tax havens. These territories are as follows: Panama, the Falkland Islands, all the Caribbean Islands and Bermuda (excluding Cuba, Haiti, the Dominican Republic, Puerto Rico and St Kitts/Nevis); in addition, the Isle of Man and the Channel Islands, Andorra, Gibraltar, Monaco, San Marino, Malta, Liechtenstein, Cyprus and Luxembourg (only in respect of Luxembourg exempt holding companies). Also included are Liberia, Mauritius and the Seychelles Republic, Jordan, the Lebanon, Bahrain, United Arab Emirates, Oman and Macao, Hong Kong, Singapore, Brunei, the Marianas, Nauru, the Solomon Islands, Vanuatu, Fiji and the Cook Islands.

In general terms, capital gains are classified into ordinary capital gains, which are those profits arising in respect of transfer of a property which has been owned for one year or less, and irregular capital gains, which are those arising from the transfer of property owned for more than one year. In accordance with the general rules, the gain or loss on transfers is paid on the difference between the higher of the transfer price or the market price and the acquisition costs which will include the price and expenses paid by the buyer.

Capital gains are considered, as has been mentioned before, one of the categories of income which is taxable by the authorities. Therefore, capital gains and losses will be assigned to the owner of the assets and there is no specific tax for capital gains, this being treated as ordinary income. As stated above, in the case of a sale of assets the capital gains or loss is the difference between the acquisition costs and the selling price. In the event of a gift or bequest, the capital gain will be the difference between the acquisition cost and the valuation of the asset under the inheritance and gift tax provisions. In addition, any increase in the taxpayer's net worth which is not justified by income during a period will be deemed to be non-justified capital gains and will be included as such in the taxable income.

Rules Applicable to Non-Residents

Non-resident individuals who derive income from or own property in Spain are required to appoint a local representative in Spain. Non-compliance with these rules may be penalised by way of a fine of between 25,000 and two million pesetas.

Buyers from non-resident owners in Spain must withhold 10 per cent of the agreed price to guarantee the eventual payment of the capital gains. This is not applicable if the property was owned for more than 20 years prior to the sale and it has not been improved during that period. As to the tax resulting from the sale of a property, there is a tax of 35 per cent applicable to the difference between the price of the acquisition and the sale. The new tax rules have eliminated a previous coefficient applied to assets owned for more than one year in order to mitigate the effects of inflation. It has introduced a variable percentage which varies according to the nature of the assets, that is there are different percentages, for example, for real estate, for shares with an official quotation etc.

8.2.3 NET WORTH TAX (*IMPUESTO SOBRE EL PATRIMONIO*)

This is an annual tax on worldwide assets in the case of residents and on assets located in Spain in the case of non-resident individuals. Net worth tax is applied in accordance with a scale which ranges from 0.2 per cent on the first 25 million up to 2.5 per cent on the excess over 1.6 billion pesetas.

There are special rules dealing with the valuation of assets and debts depending on the nature of the assets, for example real property is valued in accordance with the assets 'cadastral value,' which is the value given by the tax administration for purposes of the local property tax, or in the case of real property acquired after 1987 the value of the acquisition price for transfer tax purposes. In the case of a resident the net wealth is calculated by adding all his assets and deducting his liabilities. In addition, some property is exempted from tax, such as household furnishings and personal belongings in general.

Non-residents are subject to Spanish law in respect of their assets located in Spain. They are entitled to deduct charges or encumbrances affecting a property but they are not entitled to deduct or claim personal exemptions as in the case of residents.

Spain has entered into double taxation agreements with several countries and net worth tax has been included in these treaties. The effect will be that residents of those countries will only be taxed in the country of residence, except for those assets which are located in Spain or property effectively connected as, for example, in the case of a business located in Spain. Net worth tax provisions are included in the treaties with Belgium, Canada, Denmark, Finland, France, Germany, Hungary, Luxembourg, Morocco, the Netherlands, Norway, Poland, Romania, Sweden, Switzerland, Tunisia, the United Kingdom and the USSR (in accordance with a recent diplomatic exchange of notes, Russia assumed the benefit and liabilities in respect of the treaties signed by the USSR).

8.2.4 CORPORATION TAX (*IMPUESTO DE SOCIEDADES*)

A company is considered to be resident in Spain for corporate income tax in the following circumstances:

- if the registered office or its management office is in Spain
- if the company has been incorporated in accordance with Spanish law.

If the above criteria are not met it will be presumed that the company is a non-resident company. It should be noted that not only companies in the strict commercial sense are liable to tax under income but also partnerships and other business associations (see Chapter 3).

Corporation tax is applicable to resident and non-resident companies which carry on business in Spain. Some resident companies are 'tax transparent', that is, their income is apportioned among the members as discussed previously under 8.2.1 (A1), as for example, in the case of the European Economic Interest Groupings (EEIGs).

The tax base for corporation tax is the income obtained by the company which in the case of resident companies, includes all worldwide income, but tax credits are available for taxes paid abroad. Certain expenditure is deductible from the income as, for example, taxes paid to regional or local governments, salaries, provision for losses etc.

The corporate income tax rate is currently 35 per cent. The tax rate is applicable to the tax base provided by the profits plus capital gains plus all other income obtained by the company less the losses carried forward from prior years. The result is the gross tax payable. It must be taken into account that there are several types of expenditure which may be deductible from the profits, for example, operating costs relating to the improvement of the company's fixed assets. In general expenditure is deductible for corporate income tax purposes provided it is recorded in the accounts and have some supporting documentation.

It must be remembered that capital gains are treated as ordinary income, the gain being understood as the amount resulting from the difference obtained between the proceeds of the sale of some assets and the cost of acquisition. However, there are certain exceptions such as, for example, if the entire proceeds are reinvested in similar types of assets within two years. In order to avoid international double taxation, deductions are allowed for those residents who obtain part of the income abroad. Spain has entered into Double Taxation Agreements (*Tratado de Doble Imposicion*), the result being that a tax credit is granted to the Spanish resident, this being equal to the tax paid abroad or the tax payable in Spain on income or capital gain obtained in the other party treaty countries. Spain has signed treaties with Germany, Belgium, Denmark, Finland, France, Japan, Morocco, Norway, Poland, Portugal and Switzerland. These treaties provide for special rules in connection with dividends, interest and royalties.

Other Taxes

Companies must also comply with the business or professional licence tax. The rules in connection with this tax (*impuesto sobre actividades economicas*) are governed by Law 39/98 and implemented by the rules of Royal Decree 1175/1990.

Furthermore, companies need to deal with withholding tax (*retenciones fiscales*). This tax is generally treated as a payment on account for the resulting corporate tax liability for the year. As a general rule, it could be stated that in respect of salaries, companies must withhold an amount which is determined by the employee's salary and the number of dependents. Withholding should also be made in respect of benefits in kind to employees (for example, cars, provision for housing, etc). Spanish companies which receive income from abroad have the option of claiming credit equal to the lesser of the amount of corporate income tax paid to the foreign government or the amount of Spanish corporate income tax payable on the foreign income. The tax treaties signed contain different provisions and therefore, each case should be considered separately. For the purposes of this work, it is useful to mention that Spain has signed treaties with Austria, Belgium, Denmark, France, Germany, Japan, Norway, the Netherlands, Poland, Portugal, Morocco, Switzerland and the United Kingdom.

Dividends from a Spanish subsidiary to its EC holding company, are tax-exempt from 1 January 1992. This rule is not applicable in respect of holding companies resident in tax havens such as Monaco, Liechtenstein, Luxembourg, etc (see 8.2.2).

Non-resident companies

Spanish law distinguishes between non-resident companies which have a permanent establishment in Spain and those which have not. In practice, a permanent establishment in Spain has been interpreted as meaning that the company has management headquarters, branch offices, or some other establishment in the country. If it is concluded that a company has a permanent establishment, it is taxed on all income resulting from such establishment, at the general rate of 35 per cent. There is a 25 per cent withholding tax on permitted profits of non-residents having a permanent establishment.

If there is no permanent establishment, there may still be some tax payable in respect of

(a)   capital gains as the result of the sale of assets in Spain;
(b)   income from property;
(c)   income for securities issued by a Spanish resident company.

The reduced rate of 25 per cent is generally applicable on the above income. Non-resident companies without a permanent establishment in Spain but having some Spanish income, must appoint a resident to represent them. As a general rule, income obtained by non-resident companies, without a permanent establishment, is taxable at a rate of 25 per cent on dividends, interest, real estate rentals, royalties and fees. Capital gains are taxed at 35 per cent whether or not they relate to a permanent establishment. In any event, it must be remembered that where there are double taxation agreements different rules may apply.

In addition to the distinction between permanent and non-permanent establishment, there are some special rules applicable to those non-resident companies having a permanent establishment but sporadic activities. Their income may be taxed at 35 per cent, but they may apply for the application of a 25 per cent rate (which is the rate applicable for non-residents without a permanent establishment). The rules in this connection are complex and it is necessary to take into account different factors such as for example, the amounts transferred abroad, income obtained, etc. In any event, any application made will need to be submitted with supportive documentation.

Tax treaties may reduce or eliminate tax liabilities. In this connection, it is relevant to mention that Spain has signed treaties with Austria, Belgium, Brazil, Bulgaria, Canada, China, Denmark, Finland, France, Germany, Hungary, Italy, Japan, Luxembourg, Morocco, the Netherlands, Norway, Poland, Portugal, Romania, Sweden, Switzerland, Tunisia, the United Kingdom, the USA and Russia.

In connection with some of the special tax provisions, non-resident companies owning real property will be taxed at 5 per cent of the assessed price as determined by the local authorities. However, there are some exceptions, for example:

(a) foreign governments;
(b) companies which owned the property before 4 August 1990 and residents in a country having a double taxation agreement with Spain;
(c) companies whose usual activities are unrelated to the real estate in question;
(d) companies which provided details of the ultimate beneficiaries (owner(s)) to the Spanish authorities.

8.3 VALUE ADDED TAX (*IVA—IMPUESTO SOBRE EL VALOR AÑADIDO*)

8.3.1 APPLICABLE RULES

The rules applicable to VAT are contained in Law 37/1992 which complements Law 38/1992 on Special Taxes. In addition, there are other provisions implementing Law 37/92, one of the most important being Royal Decree 1624/92.

VAT is applied in respect of taxable supplies of goods and services by individuals or by companies. VAT does not apply in the Canary Islands where there is a special tax called a general indirect tax (*impuesto general indirecto Canario*).

Companies must submit VAT returns to the tax authorities and two special books must be maintained, one for invoices issued and one for invoices received. VAT rates have recently been increased in Spain in accordance with EC harmonisation measures on VAT (EC Directives 680/91, on the legal regime of transactions among EC members, 77/92 on harmonisation of VAT rates with a different rate and EC Regulation 218/92 on co-operation for the administration of VAT). EC Directive 77/92 sets up a general rate for EC countries which should be 15 per cent or above, permits member states to determine the reduced rate applicable to social or cultural goods or services, and allows them to maintain zero rates in some cases. In respect of the latter, Spain has maintained some exemptions, for example, in the case of educational services carried out by private or public organisations and also those carried out by individuals who are duly registered for tax purposes (*Impuesto Sobre Actividades Economicas*).

8.3.2 APPLICABLE RATES

There are three basic rates of VAT which are as follows:
1. Standard rate 15 per cent: this is the general rate unless the goods or services are included in a list with a different rate.
2. Lower rate 6 per cent: this is applicable to some goods or services which include, *inter alia*, the import or export of the following goods within the European Community:
   (a) food products with the exclusion of some drinks, including alcoholic drinks. In this respect 6 per cent is applicable, for example, to mineral water;
   (b) products used for the production of the above;
   (c) seeds, fertilizer, herbicides used in agriculture, forestry or cattle ranching excluding machinery or tools;
   (d) pharmaceutical products for veterinary use;
   (e) objects manufactured for the use in respect of human or animal disability (including spectacles and contact lenses);
   (f) health goods, material or equipment used in the prevention, diagnosis or treatment of human or animal illnesses;
   (g) garages and outbuildings which are transferred with property (this is not applicable to business premises).
In respect of services the reduced rate of 6 per cent is applicable to:
   (a) the transport of passengers and luggage;
   (b) hotel, camping, restaurants (excluding five star hotels, restaurants with three, four or five stars as well as some

other services like live shows, discotheques, etc);
(c)   services of artistes, directors and technicians provided for cinema and theatre;
(d)   cleaning services provided for streets, gardens and public parks;
(e)   services provided in respect of fairs and commercial shows;
(f)   amateur sporting events;
(g)   funeral services; and
(h)   health and dental services which are not exempted from VAT.

3. Lowest rate 3 per cent: this rate is applicable to the following goods:
(a)   food such as bread, milk, cheese, eggs, vegetables and fruit;
(b)   books, newspapers and magazines (see below);
(c)   specially adapted for the disabled and other means of transport such as wheelchairs;
(d)   prosthesis for disabled people.

With reference to the reduced rates, the law has been further implemented by a resolution dated 4 March 1993 (*Dirección General Tributos*). For example, in connection with the application of the reduced rate of 3 per cent for prosthesis, these are defined as external objects designed to replace totally or partially a limb which has been removed or is not functioning. It includes within this concept any instrument which may be introduced inside the body for structural or functional reasons. In respect of books, newspapers and magazines, the 3 per cent rate applies when the income obtained in respect of advertising does not reach 75 per cent of the total income; if the advertising income is 75 per cent or over, the 15 per cent rate will be applicable. It has been determined that the 3 per cent rate will be applicable if these publications are sold together with other products such as records, videos or similar products, provided that the cost is not more than 50 per cent of the usual sale price to the public.

8.3.3   EXEMPTIONS FROM VAT

The following goods and services are exempt:
(a)   postal services;
(b)   hospital services and medical assistance provided by

      public or private organisations;

(c)   supply of blood and other human organs for medical or research services;

(d)   services provided by orthodontists;

(e)   goods and services provided by social security;

(f)   services provided by private or public institutions in respect of social assistance activities such as protection of children and young people; services to disabled, retired or people with special needs; alcoholics, drug addicts and ex-convicts, etc;

(g)   educational services. In this respect a resolution of 4 May 1993 specified that these services have to be understood as those provided for children and young people and will include university studies (including post-graduate studies, language teaching and training). This category does not include services provided by driving schools or sports activities provided by other organisations which are not educational institutions. Furthermore, the new rules under the resolution of 4 March 1993 state that the official recognition of or authorisation granted to an institution is a pre-condition for exemption of tax in the event of the regional legislation requiring this. If the regional community (*Comunidad Autonoma*) rules do not include this requirement, the exemption from VAT is decided taking into the account the kind of activities carried out by each specific organisation. If it is required that those activities are the teaching (wholly or mainly) of a subject studied in the curriculum, the exemption position will be decided in accordance with the legislation of the regional community or the national legislation as applicable.

    In addition to the above basic rates and exemptions, the law also contains special regulations in respect of some specific activities (art 120 of the Law). The activities included, *inter alia* are:

- agriculture, cattle rearing and fishing;
- secondhand goods;
- works of art, antiques and collectors' items; and
- travel agencies etc.

8.4   MUNICIPAL AND REGIONAL TAXES

Various types of municipal fees (*tasas*) are charged in respect of public services or use of public property. As to the municipal taxes, the most important ones are those in connection with the ownership of property and with undertaking business activities.

Taxes chargeable in connection with real property are based on valuations fixed by the administration and these are charged annually. This is different from the tax on the increase in value of the land (*arbitrio de plusvalia*), which is charged on the difference in value between the acquisition value of the property and the value at the time of the sale. This tax is based not only on the increase in, value, but also on the length of time between the purchase and the sale. The tax relating to economic activities (*impuesto sobre actividades economicas*) is an annual tax applied in connection with business, professional and artistic activities. Applicable rates are fixed in accordance with several factors such as the type of activity, the number of employees etc.

In accordance with Spanish legislation, the autonomous regions may be entitled to levy their own taxes and also deal with the administration of national taxes. In practice they deal with the administration of several taxes, such as the net worth tax, inheritance and gift tax, and transfer tax. Further, some regions have agreed some regulations with the central government as to the implementation and collection of taxes, as, in the case of the Basque Country, the Canary Islands, and Ceuta Melilla.

By way of summary, it should be stated that there are tiers which may be distinguished in connection with taxes, the central government, the regions and the local authorities. This distinction is relevant not only as far as the collection of taxes is concerned but also in connection with the system for tax appeals provided under art 24 (1) of the Constitution. Under this system, a taxpayer has access to administrative and judicial appeal systems.

8.5   TAXPAYER REMEDIES

Article 24.1 of the Constitution states that every person has the right to obtain protection in the exercise of his legitimate rights and interests and that in no case should he go undefended. Accordingly, taxpayers may appeal against the decision of tax authorities. Remedies must be sought through administrative channels first and failing these, the taxpayer may initiate legal proceedings before the Superior Court (*Tribunal Superior*) in the autonomous region if the claim does not exceed three million pesetas, or before the National Court (*Audiencia Nacional*) in Madrid if the claim exceeds this amount. Provided that the claim exceeds 500,000 pesetas, it may eventually reach the Supreme Court, the court of last resort.

9
DEBT AND INSOLVENCY

9.1 GENERAL PRINCIPLES ON LIABILITIES

The main principles of Spanish Law on liabilities are contained in the Civil Code. Article 1911 established the general rule that the debtor is liable in respect of his obligations and that this will affect all the debtor's assets including future ones. Article 1089 states the sources of the obligations as being the law and contracts as clearly intended by the parties concerned. In addition, liabilities also arise from negligent actions or omissions. According to art 1156, obligations are satisfied when there is payment or fulfilment of the obligation agreed. Breach of an obligation gives rise to liability to pay compensation in respect of the damage if there has been negligence or intentional non-compliance with the obligation, or delay in compliance with the obligation.

9.2 PERSONAL GUARANTEES AND OTHER SECURITIES

In addition to the provisions dealing with the general principles of the debtor's liability, the parties to an agreement may request additional guarantees in order to ensure that an obligation will be fulfilled. Spanish law makes a distinction between personal guarantees (*garantías personales*) and other securities (*garantías reales*).

9.2.1 PERSONAL GUARANTEES

This type of guarantee is described in art 1822 of the Spanish Civil Code, which deals with one specific contract (*fianza*). By entering into this kind of guarantee, a guarantor undertakes to pay on behalf of a third party in the event of this third party not complying with an obligation. The obligation in this case depends on a principal debt and cannot exist without a valid principal obligation (art 1824 of the Civil Code). The effect of these kinds of guarantee is that the guarantor must fulfil the obligation if the principal debtor does not. In accordance with art 1839 of the Civil Code, after effecting payment on behalf of the debtor, the guarantor acquires all the rights of the creditor, including the right to demand payment of the total amount due plus legal interest from the time that the debtor was notified of the payment, in addition to expenses, if any, plus damages if there is any cause for these, for example, in the case of negligence.

This kind of guarantee exists only as long as the principal obligation is discharged at the same moment (art 1847 of the Civil Code), eg by payment of the principal debt, set-off etc.

9.2.2 OTHER SECURITIES

The granting of certain securities will ensure that payment of a debt will be made by selling some specific assets of the debtor. Two of the most important types of security under Spanish legislation are pledge (*Prenda*) and mortgage (*Hipoteca*).

Pledge

By this contract, the debtor grants possession of the assets to the pledgee or to a third party, if the parties have so agreed. There is also the possibility of a pledge without transferring possession of the charged assets in accordance with the Law of 16 December 1954. Some assets which may be charged in this way, are an expected harvest of the year of the execution of the agreement, specified machinery, goods and other raw materials which are kept in a warehouse etc.

Mortgage

A charge by way of a mortgage may affect movable or immovable property. In the case of movable property, the mortgagor retains possession of the assets. It is established law that a mortgage may be created on motor vehicles, including lorries, tractors, aeroplanes and similar assets registered in Spain, as well as industrial machinery.

In order to be valid and enforceable, the grant should be by means of a public deed (*escritura publica*) which is then registered at the relevant registries.

Mortgage of real estate (Hipoteca inmobiliaria): The creation of a mortgage will protect a creditor in the event of the debtor's default, as he can recoup payment from the proceeds of the sale of the property. The basic rules dealing with this matter are contained in the Civil Code and the laws on mortgage (*Ley Hipotecaria* and *Reglamento Hipotecario*). A mortgage is created by means of a deed executed before a public notary and duly registered at the Land Registry. The owner of the real estate retains title and can continue using the property without restriction so that, for example, he may rent out the property and keep the rents obtained.

Some of the basic characteristics of a mortgage are as follows:

(1) The mortgage is accessory to the principal obligation so that the extinction of the principal obligation also extinguishes the mortgage.

(2) The mortgage is created to secure a specific debt, that is a defined sum of money which has to be clearly stated in the deed. The mortgage must result in a charge over specific property, or properties, each or all of which must clearly be identified and defined in accordance with the records at the Land Registry.

(3) In addition to the principal amount due, the rate of interest should be ascertained or ascertainable.

As a guideline, a mortgage deed will normally include, *inter alia*, the following clauses:

(a) clear identification of the parties and the capacity in which they are acting (i.e. whether under power of attorney, on their own account etc.);

(b) details of the property to be charged;

(c) particulars of the debt, including the principal sum and interest rates applicable;

(d) particulars of repayments;

(e) consequences of late payment;

(f) circumstances as to when full payment will immediately fall due;

(g) particulars of the legal mortgage created on the property as security for payment of the debt;

(h)   covenants by the mortgagor;

(i)   applicable law and jurisdiction.

General Guidelines: In order to have a valid and enforceable mortgage, those intending to create a mortgage as a security should ensure compliance with the formalities (as stated under 9.2) and payment of the relevant taxes. It should be remembered that some time will elapse between the execution of the notarial deed and its registration, and during the interval, the property will still be registered at the Land Registry in the name of the registered owner as free of charges with the result that in practice, the mortgagor may sell the property to a third party who acquires it in good faith. The third party's title will not be affected by the mortgage if he registers the transfer of title before the mortgagee registers the mortgage granted in his favour.

The risk of this happening will be reduced as the result of Royal Decree No 1558/92, which amends the Notarial and Mortgage Regulations (*Reglamentos Notarial e Hipotecario*). The new rules, which came into force 6 August 1993, aim to give more certainty to those executing a deed transferring real property or creating a charge against real property by establishing a close collaboration between public notaries and the Land Registry. Public notaries must now obtain the property's details from the Land Registry within four days prior to the execution of a deed transferring the title or creating a charge on the property. Furthermore, the notary must forward by fax a copy of the deed to the Land Registry, if an interested party so requests. The deed must still be submitted for registration, as the new rules expressly provide that on receipt of the fax there will be a provisional registration which will last for ten days only and will be cancelled if within this period of time the authentic deed is not presented to the Land Registry.

9.3   BUSINESS INSOLVENCY

The rules dealing with business insolvency are contained in the Code of Commerce, the Code of Civil Procedure, the Law of 26 July 1992 on the suspension of payments and the Criminal Code. In addition, the general rules applicable to the procedure in bankruptcy of individuals are applicable as secondary rules.

Article 1318 of the Civil Procedure Code states that the rules relating to the insolvency of a business apply to those within the category of businessmen as defined in art 1 of the Commercial Code, that is, individuals who normally carry out business activities, having the legal capacity to do so, and commercial companies.

Those whose insolvency is of a temporary nature may resort to the procedure for a suspension of payments (*suspension de pagos*), whereas those affected by an irreversible insolvency will need to proceed through the rules provided for definitive insolvency (*Quiebra*).

9.3.1 SUSPENSION OF PAYMENTS (*SUSPENSION DE PAGOS*)

Under the rules dealing with the suspension of payments contained in the law dated 26 July 1922 and the Code of Commerce, an individual businessman or company may apply for a suspension of payments, the aim being to try to reach an agreement with the creditors. As opposed to insolvency, which ends the life of the company or marks the end of the commercial activities of the individual businessman, suspension of payments will result in a re-negotiation of the payments including rescheduling the interest resulting from the debt.

Articles 870–873 of the Commercial Code establish the requirements which need to be complied with in order to apply for a suspension of payments. These may be summarised as follows:

(1) The debtor must be an individual businessman or company.
(2) The application must be submitted by the debtor.
(3) The debtor must have sufficient assets for payment of its debts, or be able to provide a guarantor to make up the shortfall.
(4) The debtor must be unable to fulfil his obligations on the date on which they are due for payment.
(5) The debtor must submit his application in accordance with the formalities established by the law.

The Code of Commerce and the Law of 1922 set up a specific procedure for the declaration of the suspension of payments, which may be summarised as follows:

(1) The application should be supported by the accounts,

details of creditors, a proposal for payment of the debts and, in the case of limited companies, there must be a resolution passed by the board of directors.

(2)   The petition is submitted to the court of first instance (*Juez de Primera Instancia*), and the judge will examine the petition and appoint officials (*Interventores*) to inspect the books and prepare a report to the court on the business and the claims of creditors.

(3)   The judge determines whether the insolvency is temporary or permanent. When the suspension of payments is held to be permanent the effect will be that of definitive insolvency.

Where the court grants the debtors' petition for a declaration of suspension of payments it will notify the courts in other areas where the merchant or company has any branches or representative offices. The court order must also be duly registered in the Commercial Registry and at the Land Registry if the debtor is the owner of any real property.

9.3.2   INSOLVENCY (*Quiebra*)

A declaration of insolvency follows an application to court made by the creditors or by the insolvent person or company.

The petition submitted by the insolvent person or company comply with the Code of Commerce, which requires it to be supported by the accounts and a report on the causes of the insolvency, and this documentation should be duly signed by a representative of the company in question. The creditors can petition on the grounds that there are not sufficient assets for payment which has been requested and ordered by the court or where the creditors provide evidence of outstanding obligations which the debtor has been generally unable to satisfy.

Proceedings initiated by the creditors may be opposed by the debtor, and if the judge rejects the petition of the creditor or creditors the debtor may have a claim for compensation. If the judge declares an insolvency of a debtor this has the following effects:

(1)   The insolvent businessman or company loses control of the administration of his assets.

(2)   The insolvent merchant or company may not engage in trade.

(3)   Any business activities carried out after the time of the

declaration of the insolvency will be null and void.

9.3.3 INSOLVENCY PROCEEDINGS

The court which normally has jurisdiction to deal with these insolvency proceedings is the court of first instance of the businessman or of the company's registered office. In addition to the debtor and creditors, the other parties involved in these proceedings are the receivers (*síndicos*) who have the function of administering the assets and are nominated at the first creditors' meeting. Article 1346 of the Civil Code Procedure requires three receivers to be nominated. There is also a special official (*comisario*) who is appointed by the judge, who must submit to the judge a list of the creditors and the business documentation in preparation for the first creditors' meeting. This official also intervenes in the administration of the insolvent businessman or company, for example, in connection with urgent sales or necessary expenses to maintain the assets.

The aim of the procedure is to satisfy the claims of the creditors, and therefore assets administered by the receivers are finally liquidated and the debts paid in accordance with the priority of the existing claims. As a general rule, art 1926 of the Civil Code and arts 912, 913 and 914 of the Commercial Code give some guidelines as to preferential claims. Claims are divided between those which must be paid after liquidation of the bankrupt estate and those which must be paid with the proceeds of the sale of real property. The order to follow in respect of the former group is as follows:

(a) preferential creditors, including claims relating to the maintenance of the family and payment of salaries and social payments;

(b) creditors having a preferential claim in accordance with the Commercial Code (for example, commission agents);

(c) secured claims on the grounds of securities such as a mortgage;

(d) creditors having claims contained in public deeds or other commercial instruments;

(e) creditors whose claims arise out of commercial transactions;

(f) creditors whose claims arise out of civil contracts.

As to the creditors with claims to be paid out of the sale of real property, they will be ranked in accordance with the dates of their documentation.

9.3.4 TYPES OF INSOLVENCY

The judge dealing with the proceedings will decide on the basis of the evidence provided by the accounts and other documentation whether the insolvent businessman has committed fraud. If the judge concludes that there is sufficient evidence of fraud he will give the necessary instructions to initiate criminal proceedings.

It should be noted that there is a general principle that the insolvent estate includes not only those assets that were in the debtor's possession at the time of the declaration of the insolvency. It follows that transactions occurring before the declaration of insolvency may be declared void if found to be fraudulent. The transactions listed in art 8080 of the Commercial Code are *presumed* to be fraudulent and therefore void. They include gifts of real property and transactions involving real property made to satisfy debts whose payment was not due at the time of the declaration of insolvency. The general view of the courts is that transactions entered into with the sole aim of defrauding creditors are void.

In addition to fraudulent insolvency, Spanish law also makes provision for cases of negligent insolvency under arts 888 and 889 of the Commercial Code, eg where the losses resulted from gambling. Article 8887 of the Commercial Code, also considers the possibility of an accidental insolvency, that is where insolvency takes place only as a result of misfortune in spite of good commercial administration.

In deciding on the type of insolvency, among the factors which will be considered are (art 1138, Commercial Code):

(a) the conduct of the insolvent party;
(b) the accounts documentation;
(c) the report on the direct causes of the insolvency.

9.4 BANKRUPTCY

9.4.1 GENERAL PRINCIPLES

Non-businessmen facing an insolvency situation are subject

to different rules to those stated under Business Insolvency in 9.3. The rules applicable for non-businessmen are contained in the Civil Code and the Civil Procedure Code. For example, art 1912 of the Civil Code states that the debtor can request from his creditors a reduction of the debt (*quita*) an extension in respect of payment of the same (*espera*), or negotiate both arrangements at the same time. Article 1130 of the Civil Procedure Code states that those who are non-businessmen may make such arrangements with the creditors through the court before insolvency proceedings take place. The application should contain details of the creditors together with details of the claims and details of the debtor's assets and their estimated value. The judge will notify the creditors and a general meeting will take place in accordance with the details provided by the Civil Procedure Code. For quorum purposes at least three-fifths of the creditors should be present at the meeting. If there is no quorum or there is no approval from two-thirds of the creditors attending the meeting, the proposal of the debtor is taken to have been rejected (art 1142 of the Civil Procedure Code).

9.4.2 BANKRUPTCY PROCEEDINGS (*CONCURSO DE ACREEDORES*)

These proceedings can be initiated by the debtor or by his creditors. In the former case jurisdiction belongs to the court of first instance in the area of the debtor's address, and in the latter case there is jurisdiction in any court dealing with the enforcement of the judgment.

If the debtor initiates legal proceedings, he should submit details of his assets including a valuation, particulars of the claims including deatils of the creditors and a report stating the cause leading to the initiation of the proceedings. If proceedings are initiated by one or more creditors, they need to provide evidence that there are two or more judgments passed against the same debtor and that there are insufficient assets to cover the debts. If the judge agrees that these proceedings should continue, the debtor ceases to have the power to deal with his affairs. The judge will order the freezing of the assets, the notification to the debtor of this resolution and will appoint an administrator of the estate. This administrator will continue in place and receivers will be appointed to deal with the administration. The receivers control the administration of the estate and will also be in charge of collecting all the debts due to the estate, verification of the claims and the meeting of the creditors.

The sale of the assets belonging to the debtor's estate must be carried out in accordance with the rules applicable to executory proceedings (art 1326 of the Civil Procedure Code). Preferential claims guidelines are contained in art 1268, which classify the claims as follows:

(a) claims relating to personal work and food, also creditors relating to funeral expenses;
(b) claims of those having mortgage deeds and pledges;
(c) creditors with claims stated in public notarial deeds in accordance with their dates;
(d) claims which are not included in any of the above.

In all cases, after the claims have been established, the creditors and the debtor may come to any arrangement as they deem fit. Under the Civil Procedure Code, for the purpose of reaching this agreement, a meeting of creditors must take place. This meeting should be preceded by a notice containing details of the proposals, a copy of which has to be made available to all the creditors. Whoever makes the proposal undertakes to be responsible for the expenses of the meeting.

10
BANKING AND FINANCE

10.1 FOREIGN INVESTMENT AND EXCHANGE CONTROLS

10.1.1 APPLICABLE LEGISLATION

The relevant legislation is Law 18/1992 dealing with foreign investment, Royal Decree 671/1992 of 2 July and the resolution dated 6 July 1992 of the *Dirección General de Transacciones Externas* (DGTE) on the procedure applicable to the registration of foreign investment in Spain. EC directives on the area are the following: Directive 85/583 of 30 July 1963 related to the application of art 67 of the Treaty of Rome, Directive 86/566 of 17 November 1986, Directive 63/21 of 18 December 1962, Directive 86/566 of 17 November 1986 and Directive 88/361 of 24 July 1988 on the liberalisation of capital transfers.

10.1.2 INVESTMENT IN SPAIN

In accordance with the new rules, foreign investment is categorized as such according to the residence of the investor (not nationality, as previously). It should also include investments made by companies or their branches which are not resident in Spain, as well as those carried out by Spanish companies which are more than 50 per cent owned by foreign companies. In summary, therefore, foreign investment may be carried out in Spain by individuals non-resident in Spain, or by non-resident private companies.

Foreign states and other official government institutions require special administrative authorisation in order to be able to invest in Spain. Foreign investment may be by means of:

- Direct investment (including, for example, the ownership of 10 per cent or more of the share capital of a company)

- Investment in portfolio (including the acquisition of less than 10 per cent of the shares in a company)
- Investment in real property
- Other investment, such as investment in foundations, EEIGs, co-operatives etc.

Investment in certain undertakings, eg television, radio, air transport etc., is subject to special regulation. Liberalisation has not eliminated the requirement of registration of this foreign investment with the authorities, although it has had the result that as a general rule, there is no need for verification of investments.

10.1.3 SPANISH INVESTMENT ABROAD

This is governed by Law 18/1992, Royal Decree 672/1992 related to Spanish investment abroad, and Resolution of 7 July 1992 of the DGTE relating to the procedure for registration of Spanish investment abroad. So far as EC legislation is concerned, the following directives should be taken into account: First Council Directive of 11 May 1960 relating to the application of art 67 of the Treaty of Rome, Second Directive 63/21 of 18 December 1962, Directive 86/566 of 17 November 1986 and Directive 88/361 of 24 June 1988 dealing with the liberalisation of capital movements and the calendar establishing provisional periods in this connection.

Spanish investment abroad may be undertaken by individuals or companies resident in Spain, including branches of companies which are non-resident in Spain. The provisions of Royal Decree 672/1992 makes residence the test of such investment.

Investment abroad may take the form not only of money but also eg patents, machinery, non-distribution of dividends etc. As in the case of investment into Spain, Spanish investment abroad may be by direct investment, investment in portfolio, real estate investment and so forth. The general rule is that no previous verification is required, but there are exceptions, for example, if the investment is 250 million pesetas or more, when the investment is going to be effected in a country which is classified as 'fiscal paradise'. As a general rule, Spanish investment abroad should be registered with the Minister of Economic Affairs at the Registry of Investment.

10.2 BANKING SECTORS

10.2.1 BANK OF SPAIN

The Bank of Spain is the central bank in charge of carrying out the monetary policies decided by the Ministry of Economic Affairs and the Treasury. In addition, it has the power to control the banking system. Its legal position derives from the Law of 14 April 1962 and the Decree of 7 June 1962, together the regulations implementing them. The Bank of Spain is empowered:

- to issue coins and notes
- to regulate and control monetary circulation, and
- in general, to develop monetary policies.

In respect of other banks, the Bank of Spain exercises disciplinary and supervisory faculties based on the law of 29 July 1988 (*Ley de Disciplina e Intervencion de las Entidades de Credito*). In order to achieve these objectives, the bank issues its own regulations (circulars) which have to be adopted and implemented by other Spanish banks. Some of the most important regulations are those relating to Users' Complaints Procedure (Order of 3 March 1987, Circular 24/87 and Circular 8/90).

10.2.2 SPANISH BANKS

Spanish banks are classified into public banks and private banks. Public banks are those which have a majority public ownership; they include the official credit institutions, the Banco Exterior and the postal savings bank. Private banks are those carrying out banking activities with the authorisation of the government. The five largest Spanish banks are Banco Bilbao Vizcaya, Banco Central Hispano Americano, Banco de Santander and Banco Espanol de Credito and Banco Popular. Incorporation in Spain is governed by Royal Decree 1444/88, which includes the requirements for opening foreign banking establishments and subsidiaries of foreign banks which also must comply with the same requirements as the Spanish banks.

In addition to the above, there are other banks which play an important role within the Spanish banking system, the savings banks (*Cajas de Ahorros*). These saving banks have gradually been allowed to carry out activities which used to be restricted to the above stated banks. Savings banks must be registered in the Commercial Registry in accordance with Law 19/89 and Regulations 1597/89. In addition to their financial activities they also have charitable and social functions. Savings banks have to comply with the administrative controls which are applicable to other credit institutions, for example annual audits of their accounts. The Spanish Confederation of Savings Banks (*Confederacion Española de Cajas de Ahorros—CECA*) is a financial institution providing saving banks with banking services in support of some of their national and international operations.

10.3　CAPITAL STANDARDS AND OTHER BANKING REGULATIONS

Spanish legislation has adopted new rules in order to achieve harmonisation with EC Directives. The new banking regulations deal primarily with solvency requirements. EC Directives 89/299, 89/646 and 89/647 deal with solvency requirements for lending institutions. Spanish legislation has implemented these directives through Law 13/1992 of 1 June (*Recursos propios y supervision en base consolidada entidades financieras*), Royal Decree 1343 of 6 November 1992 which implemented this law and further, the order of the Minister of Economic Affairs of 30 December 1992 on the rules of solvency applicable to lending institutions. These rules deal with, for example, exchange rates transactions and provide that they should have their own reserves in an amount sufficient to cover the risk undertaken. The law also lays down specific guidelines in connection with risks (Royal Decree 1343/1992 which came into force on 1 January 1993 with the exception of some provisional measures due to come into force on 4 January 1994, for example, in respect of high risk limits: art 30).

There may be some further changes implementing EC Directive 92/121 of 21 December 1992, which deals with the supervision and control of high risk operations carried out by lending institutions (*entidades de credito*). In accordance with this rule, there will be a high risk when the value of operations in relation to a client or a group of clients related *inter se*, is equivalent to or over 10 per cent of their own assets. In respect of a client or a group of clients, lending institutions will not be able to undertake risks whose value is over 25 per cent of their own assets, or 20 per cent in the case of the holding company or subsidiaries of the lending institution. This Directive has to be implemented before 1 January 1994.

Banks need to comply with good banking practices, and some operations are prohibited, for example, particular loans between institutions. In the event that a bank is facing financial difficulties, receivers may be appointed to take part in the management, or the board of directors may be replaced.

Consumers are protected in respect of their relationship with banks by general rules such as the 1984 General Consumers Protection Law (*Ley General de Defensa de los Consumidores y Usuarios*) and Law 34/88 on Advertising. Further, banks must comply with information standards in respect to customers, and there is a credit customers complaint service to handle complaints from customers. Disciplinary rules are laid down by Law 26/1988, which classifies offences as minor, serious or very serious; sanctions may be applied, which may include revoking the banking licence. In the case of very serious offences, the case will be considered by the Ministry of Economics Affairs and Finance. This Law has been further implemented by an Order dated 12 September 1989.

So far as the security markets are concerned, the basic law is Law 24/1988 and Royal Decree 291/1992. This Law set up the National Securities Exchange Commission (*commission nacional del mercado de valores*) which supervises the securities market, the Bank of Spain and the Ministry of Economic Affairs.

10.4 NEGOTIABLE INSTRUMENTS

The provisions applicable to cheques, bills of exchange and promissory notes are contained in the Law of 16 July 1985, in force from 1 January of 1986 (*Ley Cambiaria y del Cheque*) (and the rules of the Civil Procedure, eg art 1429).

10.4.1 CHEQUES

Under the 1986 Law, a cheque must contain the following
(a) the word 'cheque' written in the document;
(b) name of the person giving the instructions to pay (*librador*) and his signature;

(c)   particulars of the bank effecting the payment (*librado*)
       (this includes not only banks in the true sense but also
       savings banks);
(d)   the specified sum of money to be paid, in words and in
       figures;
(e)   date of issue of the cheque;
(f)   place of issue of the cheque;
(g)   place of payment.

If either of the two last details are not included the document
is still valid but the place of issue will be deemed to be that of the
librador (drawer) and the place of payment that of the paying bank.

Cheques may be drawn payable either to a stated payee (*a la
orden*) or it may be an open or bearer cheque (*al portador*). A
cheque may be endorsed in favour of a third party, provided that
payment is to a named payee and that it does not contain a clause
prohibiting endorsement (*no a la orden* or similar). Payment of the
cheque may be guaranteed by a third party (*aval*). The third party
providing the guarantee has the same liabilities as the drawer
issuing the cheque. The payee may claim payment of the cheque
and in the event of non-payment, is entitled to claim interest, plus
damages and costs related to the claim. A cheque is one of the
documents included in art 1429 of the Civil Code procedure as
providing sufficient evidence for starting executory proceedings
(*Juicio Ejecutivo*) requesting payment, provided that evidence is
supplied of non-payment, for example, by notarial act (*protesto*).

10.4.2   BILLS OF EXCHANGE (*LETRA DE CAMBIO*)

The new Law of 1986 introduced some important changes to
the previous provisions of the Code of Commerce. These changes
include, *inter alia*, interest for delay in payment in respect of the
guarantor's obligations which are no longer dependant on the
obligations of the principal debtor, but independent of them.

A bill of exchange contains an instruction (given by one
party (*librador*) for payment of a specified sum of money to
another (*librado*), who undertakes the obligation to pay to a third
party (*tenedor o tomador*). It must also include the date and place of
payment, and the place and date where the document was issued.
This document must be duly signed in acceptance by the person
undertaking to make the payment. A bill of exchange can also be
endorsed and the endorsement should be made in respect of the

total amount and without any conditions. Partial endorsements are void. A bill of exchange can also be assigned in favour of a third party. A third party (*Aval*) may undertake payment of the total or partial amounts due (arts 35, 36 and 37 of Law of 1986).

A bill of exchange is also one of the documents in respect of which payment may be claimed through executory proceedings in accordance with arts 1429 to 1480 of the Civil Procedure Law (*Juicio Ejecutivo*). This enables judgments to be obtained more quickly than in ordinary proceedings.

Where a bill of exchange is lost, the creditor will be able to prevent a third party from obtaining payment or recognition of his rights by initiating legal proceedings before the court having jurisdiction at the place where payment was due.

10.4.3 PROMISSORY NOTES (*PAGARE*)

A promissory note must contain the following details:

(a)   its description as such in writing i.e. *Pagare* in the text of the document;
(b)   an unconditional undertaking to make payment of a specified sum of money;
(c)   the date of payment;
(d)   the place where payment is to be made;
(e)   name of the person entitled to receive payment;
(f)   place and date of issue of the promissory note;
(g)   signature of the person issuing the promissory note.

Some rules applicable to bills of exchange are also applicable to promissory notes, in the case of endorsement, claims in respect of non-payment, clauses in respect of interest, in respect of loss of the documents and applicable legal proceedings. A promissory note's payment can be claimed through executory proceedings (art 1429.4, Civil Procedure Law), this being one of the changes introduced by the Law of 1986.

10.5   FINANCING METHODS

Banks and other financial institutions provide short, medium and long term financing to those engaged in business. The liberalisation process has resulted in new opportunities of financing for Spanish companies.

10.5.1 LOANS AND CREDITS

When a loan transaction is agreed the lender undertakes to lend a sum of money to another party, the borrower, who undertakes to repay the principal together with any agreed commission or interest. Under Spanish law banks, including saving banks and also some other bodies such as financial institutions and mortgage credit institutions, are authorised to grant loans in accordance with the regulations and applicable laws, for example, the provisions included in the Order of 12 December 1989. Loans may be granted to individuals or to companies. Interest rates may be fixed or (since 1980) floating. Floating interest rates may be based on the prime rate set by a credit institution or the market rate. However, credit institutions are not allowed to use their own prime rate for loans which they grant.

Alternatively, it may be agreed that some funds are to be available through credits which are placed in favour of the beneficiary who will draw on these as convenient. The advantage of this method is that interest is paid only on the principal amount which has been actually used. Spanish law has not specially regulated these credit operations, but their continued use has created a customary practice. Such credits may also be arranged with fixed or floating interest rates. In addition the standard clauses usually applicable to loans will apply to these credit agreements.

10.5.2 DISCOUNTING AGREEMENTS (*DESCUENTOS*)

Article 178 of the Commercial Code refers to bank operations relating to the discount of letters of credit, promissory notes and other similar instruments. In these transactions, a bank advances monies before payment is due to a creditor. Banks can then in turn, re-discount these credits to the Bank of Spain. In this kind of transaction banks will require the client to undertake to return the monies if the amounts due by the debtor are not eventually paid.

10.5.3 FACTORING

Factoring is a contract which is not expressly dealt with by Spanish legislation but is widely recognised in practice. This is basically a commercial contract. The parties to a factoring agreement are:

(a) the factoring institution, which collects credit on behalf of a creditor, assuming the risk of loss in the event of non-payment of the debtor, in return for an agreed discount and a high interest rate;

(b) the creditor (*cedente*), generally a company, which may agree to bear the risk (in which case the factoring institution will be acting as agent) or may agree that the non-payment is to be at the risk of the factoring institution;

(c) the debtor, who has agreed to the possible assignment of the debt to a third party.

Needless to say a factoring agreement is reached after long negotiations, after the factoring institutions have considered the debtor's financial position and the risk of insolvency.

Some of the rules applicable to factoring agreements are those applicable to long term financing institutions such as the Order of 13 May 1981 of the Ministry of Economic Affairs under Law 396/77.

10.5.4 LEASING

Law 26/88 states that leasing operations are those having as their purpose the assignment of the use of movable or real property acquired for such specific purpose and in accordance with a description of future use, in consideration of specified periodical payments of a specific sum of money. It is further stated that in the case of property this should be used exclusively for agriculture, fishing, industrial or commercial services or professional activities. The inclusion of a clause giving the lessee the option to purchase at the termination of the agreement is essential. The minimum period of time in respect of leasing agreements for movable property is two years. In respect of real property or industrial premises the period of time is ten years.

Law 26/88 states that only certain credit institutions are authorised to carry out leasing operations. Among these institutions are banks, including saving banks, mutual credit associations and leasing companies. Other rules should also be taken into account, for example Royal Decree 1044/89 stated that capital advisory requirements were not only needed in respect of banks and saving banks but also in respect of leasing companies, and the order dated 8 February 1991 relating to disciplinary measures is applicable to leasing companies. Leasing companies are subject to regulation. For example they must have a minimum fully paid-up capital of 500,000,000 pesetas, they must be authorised by the Ministry of Economic Affairs to carry on the activities of leasing, and they must be registered at the leasing company register with the Bank of Spain (which exercises powers of control and inspection over them) and also at the Mercantile Registry.

Leasing contracts must be in writing. There are several rules applicable to these contracts as for example Royal Decree 15/77, Decree 1669/80 and Law 26/88. These rules initially authorised leasing only in respect of certain goods such as vehicles; subsequently the leasing of real property for business purposes was authorised.

Leasing companies may enter into leasing contracts. Under a leasing contract, the lessor undertakes to acquire certain goods or property in accordance with the lessee's instructions. Possession is then given to the lessee who has the option to purchase the property at the termination of the agreement. In turn, the lessee undertakes to pay the price agreed in the leasing contract together with the value agreed should he exercise his option to purchase. In addition the lessee is liable in respect of all the expenses resulting from the use, maintenance and repair of equipment, and he assumes the risk of damage to and loss of the equipment. At the end of the agreement the lessee may exercise his option to purchase, or a new leasing agreement may be negotiated or if neither alternative is agreed the goods have to be returned to the lessor who may then lease them to another lessee.

10.6 THE STOCK EXCHANGE AND CAPITAL MARKETS

The Spanish securities market is regulated by Law 24/1988 of 28 July (*Ley del Mercado de Valores*). This law has been supplemented by other rules such as, for example, Royal Decree 116/92 dealing with letters of exchange, promissory notes and other securities which may be the object of some transactions in the securities market (*Valores Negociables*).

10.6.1 NATIONAL SECURITIES AND MARKET COMMISSION

One of the major changes introduced by this law is the creation of the National Securities Market Commission (*Comision Nacional de Valores* (CNMV)). This Commission supervises and controls the securities market. Its aims and major powers are set out in art 13 of the Securities Market Act. These are, *inter alia*, as follows:

(a)   to protect investors, to whom full information must be provided;

(b)   to ensure fair dealing in the market place;

(c)   to exercise control over the primary securities market;

(d)   to deal with the admission, suspension or exclusion of securities for transactions in the secondary market;

(e)   to advise the government and exercise disciplinary powers;

(f)   to ensure that there is correct pricing within the market.

10.6.2 PRIMARY MARKET

As a general rule, securities in the primary market are not subject to prior administrative authorisation. However, the issuer must notify the Commission. Information relating to the issue must be filed with the Commission, and a prospectus regarding the issue must be published. In addition, the Commission will need to see the issuer's auditor's report.

10.6.3 SECONDARY MARKET

The secondary market, includes Stock Exchanges, the public debt market, and any other secondary market the goverment may create with national scope and represented by accounting entries.

Stock Exchange operations are regulated by Royal Decree 1416/91. Securities companies (*Sociedades de Valores*) and agencies (*Agencias de Valores*) are the brokers able to trade securities on the Stock Exchange. These security companies and agencies must be *Sociedades Anonimas* which in addition to the normal requirements for these types of companies (see Chapter 3) need also to have their articles of association officially approved by the Ministry of Economic Affairs acting on the recommendation of the Commission. They need an initial authorised share capital of 750,000,000 pesetas for securities companies and in the case of an agency, an initial share capital of 150,000,000 pesetas. Capital must be fully paid-up at the time of incorporation of the company. There are also other legal requirements relating eg to the composition of the boards of directors. Security companies must have five directors, and agencies must have at least three directors.

There are Stock Exchanges in Madrid, Barcelona, Bilbao and Valencia. Their activities are supervised and controlled by the National Securities Exchange Commission. In addition, the Bank of Spain also has supervisory powers. Control is exercised over the permanent and indirect participants which may include, banks and savings banks, etc.

As to offences committed, these are classified into serious, very serious and minor (art 99 of the Law 24/1988) and sanctions are applied accordingly. In the case of very serious offences, directors may be removed from office for up to five years or disqualified from holding office for up to ten years. In the case of serious offences, sanctions may include suspensions for periods of up to one year and/or fines, etc. In the case of minor offences, sanctions include a fine of up to 500,000,000 pesetas. Serious offences are listed in art 99 of law 24/1988 and will include, for example, failure to audit the annual accounts, improper use of privileged information etc. Among the serious offences listed in art 100 are the failure to keep proper accounts, or to give priority to customers' interests. The minor offences under art 101 are offences of non-compliance with the provisions of the securities market.

11
ENVIRONMENT AND PLANNING

11.1 ENVIRONMENTAL PROTECTION

11.1.1 INTRODUCTION

Spanish legislation includes a variety of laws dealing with the issue of environmental protection.

National and Regional Rules: Article 45 of the Constitution provides that everyone has the right to enjoy an environment suitable for their personal development, as well as the duty to preserve it, and that public authorities must ensure a rational use of all natural resources for the purpose of protecting and improving and restoring the environment by relying on essential public co-operation.

The environment is not only protected at national level, but the regional governments also have powers to deal with this matter in their respective territories by art 148.1.3 of the Constitution.

Local Regulation: Local authorities have powers in connection with land and urban planning. They ensure that the use of buildings and dwellings and the carrying on of activities in buildings are in accordance with the principles in licences and building permits.

EC Legislation: Membership of the EC has produced a significant impact. The influence of EC legislation has gone beyond the simple implementation of Directives, as a structure has been created to deal with the protection of the environment. This is the General Secretariat of the Environment created within the Ministry of Planning in 1990 (Royal Decree 199/1990), who are responsible for the drafting of environmental legislation and plans at a national level and also for co-ordinating with European Community organisations, ensuring that EC rules are implemented in Spain.

11.1.2 APPLICABLE LEGISLATION

A wide range of matters have been included within the concept of environmental law. It is not possible in the space available to list all relevant legislation but some major areas are:

Activities causing nuisance, insalubrious, noxious and hazardous activities

These are regulated by Decree No 2414/1961 and implemented by the Order of 15 March 1963. The provisions applicable to these activities specify that those activities considered to create a nuisance are those which create noise, vibration, odours, smoke, dust or other substances. Insalubrious activities are those which might directly or indirectly harm human health. Noxious activities are those which might harm culture, forestry, livestock or fish. Hazardous activities are those relating to products which may result in serious risk of explosion, radiation, or similar risks to people or property. All these above activities are supervised by local authorities through licences which will only be granted if the established procedure is complied with. An application for a licence in the case of substantial activities needs to include a plan of the premises, buildings, agricultural activity etc. All applications must give details of the proposed activities, their anticipated consequences and the protective measures which will be taken: the order of 15 March 1963 contains detailed rules as to the application procedure. In the event of a refusal of the application, an appeal can be made to the administrative authorities. If they reject the appeal, the affected party may have recourse to the ordinary courts.

Lack of compliance with the provisions applicable will be penalised by fines, cancellation of a licence etc. depending on the seriousness of the offence.

Legislation protecting the sea and the coast

These rules are provided by the 1988 *Ley de Costas* (Law of the Coast), which became widely known in connection with building restrictions. In accordance with this Law the authorities can restrict building and control height and density within 100 metres of the high water mark. This area may be expanded by the public administration up to a maximum of another 100 metres, taking into account the particular features of the coastal area (art 23).

In accordance with Article 25 the following activities are prohibited:

(a) building construction;

(b) the construction or modification of trunk roads or highways and other heavily used roads;

(c) activities resulting in the destruction of sand deposits;

(d) elevated laying of high tension electricity cables;

(e) dumping of solid residues, garbage or waste water without purification;

(f) advertising by posters or by acoustic or audio-visual means.

Exceptionally and for reasons of public interest the Cabinet Council (*Consejo de Ministros*) may authorise the activities referred to under (a) and (b).

In any event any authorised activity must be carried out in accordance with the urban plan approved by the local authority. Planning regulations, should be checked with the local authority and also with the *Jefatura de Costas* (Coast Department) to ensure that development is legal and registered.

In addition there is a wide variety of legislation dealing with water protection, for example, Law 21/1977 on the sanctions against marine contamination from ships and boats.

Pollution

In addition to the above there is further legislation dealing with the protection of the environment and the prevention of contamination. In this respect it is important to mention the following:

- Decree No 1088/1992 of 11 September 1992 on air pollution. The aim of this Decree, which incorporates EC Directives 89/369 and 89/429 into Spanish national legislation, aims to prevent pollution from new municipal waste installations and to reduce the pollution produced by old installations

- Health Regulations on ionising radiations of 24 January 1992, implementing EC Directives 80/836 and 84/467. This Decree implements the provision of Law 25/1964 on nuclear energy. The aim of these regulations is to protect workers and the public in general from ionising radiation and from all kinds of nuclear and radioactive activities, and they contain detailed lists of the dose of exposure permissible.

Penalties for non-compliance will be imposed through fines ranging from 25,000 pesetas to 100,000,000 pesetas according to the seriousness of the offence committed.

11.2 PLANNING

11.2.1 INTRODUCTION

The right to private property is recognised by art 33 of the 1978 Spanish Constitution. Article 33 also states that this right has a social purpose which limits the content as provided by law. Therefore privately owned land must be used and developed in accordance with the law. In addition, art 148 of the Constitution gives power in connection with town planning and housing to the autonomous regions. This must be read together with Royal Decree 1/1992, a consolidated text dealing with land use and urban planning and taking as its basis the provisions of the 1976 and 1979 Land Acts (*Ley del Suelo*). In addition to national and regional regulations there is a wide range of municipal planning provisions, dealing with the classification of land, building permits etc.

11.2.2 APPLICABLE PROVISIONS

As stated above, the basic legislation concerning urban planning land classification and building activities is contained in Royal Decree number 1/1992 which consolidated the existing legislation on the matter. The law deals with a variety of matters some of which can be further implemented and developed by the autonomous regions. The most important matters dealt with by these provisions are as follows:

1. *Classification of Land*: Article 9 classifies land as urban (*Suelo Urbano*) which may be developed (*Suelo Urbanizable*) and land which may not be developed (*Suelo no Urbanizable*). The latter refers to areas which are not included in the above categories, or areas which had been listed for special protection taking into account their value for agriculture, forestry or the protection of the environment. The above classification is relevant for those municipalities where general municipal plans (*Planes Generales Municipales de Ordenacion*) are applicable.

For those municipalities where the above general municipal

plans are not applicable, land is divided into urban land and land which may not be developed. In addition, there are other provisions included in partial plans' (*Planes Parciales*). These regulations provided further details about the land which may be developed in accordance with the general municipal plans.

The right to develop thus requires compliance with the relevant rules of both the general municipal plan and the partial plans.

2. *Right to Build*: In order to exercise the right to build it is necessary to obtain a building permit. The building permit will provide details as to the date for starting and finishing the authorised works. The completion of the building works must be declared by means of a public deed (*Declaracion de Obra Nueva*) which is then registered at the Land Registry.

3. *Urban Development Plans*: Chapter 3 of the new provisions dealing with urban planning provides for a national plan, giving general guidelines which have to be taken into account by each local authority when drafting its general municipal plans. Local authorities may have partial plans to develop the general municipal plans in accordance with detailed regulations applicable to some specific areas relating to urban land or land which may be developed.

11.2.3 PRACTICAL GUIDELINES

The law on urban planning is complex and detailed. It is therefore advisable in respect of any transaction related to property rights in land to refer to the following:

- the general provision dealing with land and urban planning
- specific provisions provided by the general municipal plans
- further provisions provided by partial plans.

The above information may be obtained in the first instance by approaching the local authorities regarding applicable legislation and the plans covering the area where the property is located. When this information is obtained, the necessary permission should be obtained. Permits are obtained on compliance with certain formalities, for example, a building permit will require an architect's drawings (except in the case of some minor works). Once a building permit has been issued construction should take place in accordance with its terms. Permits which expire at the end of a period are not always renewed, or may be revoked on the grounds of illegality. The expiration of a permit brings about the expiration of the right to build.

Provided that all the relevant rules have been complied with, so that construction has taken place in accordance with the licence granted by the municipal authorities, the building may be suitable for human habitation. A special certificate is granted confirming this (*Cedula de Habitabilidad*).

When a construction has taken place with a view of carrying on business activities, in addition to licence and building permits legislation other legal requirements should be taken into account depending on the circumstances, for example the provisions relating to nuisance, insalubrious, noxious and hazardous activities (see 11.1.2).

LEGISLATION TABLE

INDEX